D0836254

Controversies in Sociology
edited by
Professor T. B. Bottomore and Dr Michael Mulkay

1

Social Theory and Political Practice

Social Theory and Political Practice

by

BRIAN FAY

Department of Philosophy
Wesleyan University, Connecticut

London

George Allen & Unwin Ltd

Ruskin House Museum Street

First published in 1975

ISBN 0 04 300047 9 hardback
0 04 300048 7 paperback

Printed in Great Britain
in 10/11 pt Times Roman type
by Willmer Brothers Limited, Birkenhead

Acknowledgements

This book owes a great deal to a number of people, but to these in particular: John Plamenatz, my former teacher who has discussed, and sometimes disagreed with me on, these matters for the past six years, and who read the manuscript with his usual care and insight; Michael Brody, my student who has contributed enormously to the development of my ideas these past two years, not least by refusing to be bull-dozed; Louis Mink, my philosophical patriarch who taught me the philosophy of social science while I was ostensibly teaching a class in it with him; Tom Bottomore and Michael Mulkay, the editors of this series who made a number of helpful suggestions; Don Moon, my dear friend and fellow philosopher whose ideas and criticism run through every page of this book; and lastly, to my wife Ingrid, who so warmly supported me when I was first hesitatingly trying to work out these ideas.

I would like to dedicate this book to her.

Contents

1

Introduction: Theory and Practice

This is a short book which tries to accomplish two things at once: on the one hand it is intended as an overview of the principal current ideas about the relationship between social theory and political practice; and, on the other, it is an attempt to develop a critical stance towards these ideas, with the hope of providing a new and more satisfactory account of this relationship. These two aims are not unrelated to one another. As will become apparent in the text, one of the major themes that emerges from the description I give of the main positions which have been taken on this matter is the intimate connection that exists between the ideas that we have and the sort of life that we lead, and it is in the light of this that I could not maintain a neutral attitude towards the ideas I had to discuss. What is at stake in these matters is not merely certain academic questions about how to conduct social inquiry, but also socially relevant ideas which have a direct bearing on the question of how our social life is to be conducted.

The general question with which this book is concerned is how our knowledge about social life affects, or ought to affect, our living of it.[1] Normally these notions are not considered together: on the one side there is social theory which seeks to *explain*

[1] The question which is dealt with here is thus a special case of the more general problem of how knowledge is related to action. For a historical review of how this general problem has been formulated and treated since the Greeks, cf. N. Lobkowicz, *Theory and Practice*. (Full references to works cited are provided in the Bibliography.)

social behaviour, on the other there is political philosophy which proposes ways in which our social theories may be used to *change* social behaviour, but no necessary connection is thought to exist between them. One is quite accustomed to seeing sharp divisions being drawn between knowledge and the uses of knowledge, between questions in the philosophy of social science and those in political philosophy, between scientific activity and political activity, and between theory and practice.

These are, of course, not all distinctions of the same type, but they are all rooted in the conventional approach which separates 'theoretical matters' from 'practical matters', which drives a wedge between questions about what is the case from questions about what ought to be done. One of the central claims of this book is that as long as this conventional approach is employed *both* our understanding of the nature of social theory *and* our understanding of the way in which such theory is related to practical action will be seriously impaired; moreover – in the light of my remarks in the first paragraph – it is also one of the chief arguments of the book that these misunderstandings themselves will have important political consequences.

Even on an introductory and intuitive level, however, the neat divisions which are usually drawn or assumed in analysis might sound somewhat implausible: for men are not generally schizoid in their thought, such that they view social life in one way when they wish to study it, and in a quite different way when they come to questions as to how the knowledge they have gained is relevant to the practical problems which confront them. But, of course, the issue is not simply whether certain ideas are interrelated, but whether they are *necessarily so,* and, if so, *in precisely what ways.* And it is just this notion of necessity which modern conventional wisdom denies; for it distinguishes between the two different roles a man may play – a scientist who is a seeker of truth, and a political actor engaged in practical activity – with the idea being that in principle these roles are distinct even though in practice they may be interrelated in some way. It is just this bit of 'common sense' that I hope to undermine and to replace with an account of social science which starts from a radically different premise, namely, one which is rooted in an explicit theory of how this social science is related to political practice.

The account to which I am referring is the 'critical model' which I develop in Chapter 5. But prior to this I also give an account of two other, more familiar, models of social science, the positivist model and the interpretive model. Actually, given what I have just asserted – that implicit in ideas about the nature of social theory is a latent conception of how this theory is related to practice – it will be necessary for me to give somewhat different descriptions of these more familiar models than are usually given. The reason for this is that the conventional descriptions, which fail to make explicit this latent conception, are seriously inadequate, and this inadequacy I hope to have overcome.

This leads me to say something about the term 'positivist social science'. I use this term to refer to that metatheory of social science which is based on a modern empiricist philosophy of science often referred to as the hypethetico-deductive model of science. Its principal contemporary exponents are Carl Hempel,[2] Karl Popper,[3] and Ernst Nagel,[4] though there are, of course, from certain points of view, important differences among them. For my purposes there are four essential features of this metatheory: first, drawing on the distinction between discovery and validation, its deductive-nomological account of explanation and concomitant modified Humean interpretation of the notion of 'cause'; second, its belief in a neutral observation language as the proper foundation of knowledge; third, its value-free ideal of scientific knowledge; and fourth, its belief in the methodological unity of the sciences. There are a number of secondary claims which are made by this model – e.g. having to do with the nature of theories – as well as an entire epistemology and metaphysics rooted in a philosophy of meaning which underlie and support this metatheory, but it is not necessary for me to detail these here. At this point all I wish to do is to locate the positivist model; how I understand its four central features, and how they comprise a model of social inquiry, will only become clear in the course of the argument presented in Chapter 2.[5]

In connection with the use of the term 'positivist social

[2] Cf. *Aspects of Scientific Explanation.*

[3] Cf. *The Logic of Scientific Discovery* and *Conjectures and Refutations.*

[4] Cf. *The Structure of Science.*

[5] Cf. the Appendix at the end of this chapter for a discussion of how another, Kuhnian, metatheory of science relates to all this.

science', there is also a possible confusion in the term I use to characterise its political theory, namely the term 'policy science'. This is an ambiguous term, not because I use it in a variety of ways, but because it has two closely related meanings only one of which is relevant to my purposes. Sometimes[6] by a 'policy science' is meant that process of analysis by which the various consequences of particular courses of action are spelled out in terms of their monetary costs and benefits so that a decision-maker may be well informed as to the possible outcomes of his alternatives. A policy science in this sense is intended, to use the current jargon, to 'map the decision space' in which the policy maker is going to act. This is *not* the meaning of 'policy science' as I use the term in this book.

The other meaning of 'policy science' which *is* how I use the term here is that set of procedures which enables one to determine the technically best course of action to adopt in order to implement a decision or achieve a goal. Here the policy scientist doesn't merely *clarify* the possible outcomes of certain courses of action, he actually *chooses* the most efficient course of action in terms of the available scientific information. In this regard, the policy scientist really is a type of social engineer who makes instrumental decisions on the basis of the various laws of science – in this instance, social science – which are relevant to the problem at hand. The policy engineer, if I may use this phrase, is one who seeks the most technically correct answer to political problems in terms of available social scientific knowledge.

With these perhaps somewhat obscure remarks out of the way, I think the body of the text is more or less self-explanatory. In section 2.1 I set out a quite common notion of how the knowledge gained from a social science positivistically conceived is to be applied to social life, and then I attempt in section 2.2 to show that these two ideas – an idea of science and an idea of its use – are conceptually linked, that, in other words, it is no accident that the positivistic model leads to what I call a technological view of politics. My general claim in section 2.2 is that, contrary

[6] Cf. Harold Lasswell, 'Policy Sciences', in the *International Journal of the Social Sciences*. The history of this conception of the notion 'policy science' is found in the development of welfare economics and in the wartime problems of source allocation. For a good summary, cf. A. R. Prest and R. Turvey, 'Cost-Benefit Analysis: A Survey', in *Surveys of Economic Theory*.

to the value-free ideal of the positivist tradition, the scientific enterprise understood positivistically contains within itself an implicitly instrumentalist notion of how theory and practice are related, and that, with regard to the social sciences, there is consequently an implied *political theory* as an element in its account of what it means to understand social life.

It ought to be clear from what I have just said, as well as in the actual argument of section 2.2, that even though I concentrate on the case of social science, the general argument that I make does *not* rest on a claim that the social sciences are ethically biased in ways in which the natural sciences are not. Quite the contrary; the argument that I adduce there is equally applicable to both enterprises. Of course, this does not preclude the possibility that the social sciences *might* be value non-neutral in ways which the natural sciences are not, but that is another question which I do not examine.

Moreover, it should be noted, my claim as to the ideological content of a model of science is not one of those most often heard in discussions about values in the social sciences:[7] it is *not* the claim that certain values (such as simplicity, elegance, systematic integrity, quantitativeness, etc.) are inherent in the very process of scientific analysis itself; *nor* is it the claim that a scientist's values will help to determine what questions he asks, what areas he studies, etc. (so that, e.g., an economist analyses the conditions of growth because he holds the value that material enrichment is a good); *nor* is it the claim that it is only by agreeing to certain value-judgements that one can accept the truth claims of a particular social scientist (so that, e.g., it is only by making the judgement as to the goodness of the communist state that one can accept the Marxian analysis of modern society). None of the arguments and counter-arguments about these traditional claims is what I have in mind when I discuss the question of the ideological bias of a model of social science.

The reason for this is that all of these claims concern the role of values *within* the framework of scientific activity, whereas I am concerned with the role which values have as part of the conceptual framework which defines what it is to have real, i.e. scientific, knowledge about some phenomenon. I am claiming

[7] For these, cf. the recent collection edited by G. Riley, *Values, Objectivity, and the Social Sciences.*

that implicit in the theories of knowledge which I examine (the positivist in Chapter 2, the interpretive in Chapter 4, and the critical in Chapter 5) is a certain conception of the relation between knowledge and action, and that such a conception, when elaborated in the context of social life, is a political theory. It is in this, I think much deeper, way that I argue that there is an ideological content to what I call models of social science.[8]

In Chapter 3 I set out some criticisms of the positivist view, moving from a consideration of its ideas about theory and practice in sections 3.1 and 3.2, to a consideration of its views about the nature of social theory in section 3.3. In Chapter 4 I develop, and then criticise, an alternative model of social science which contains within it an alternative view about how social knowledge is to be translated into action. I do this for two reasons: the first is to highlight the assumptions of the positivist model; the second is to lay the groundwork for the critical model which I outline in Chapter 5.

It is in Chapter 5 that all of the general points I have been making while examining the problems of social theory and politics in the positivist and interpretive models are taken into explicit account in the construction of a model of social science. I believe that this model, at least in the way I argue for it and explicate it, is novel, and also that it goes some way beyond the current discussions in the philosophy of social science as found in the analytic tradition. Moreover, in keeping with my appreciation of the political significance of theories about social science, I also hope that this critical model establishes the foundation for a type of inquiry that is *truly* liberating.

[8] It should also be stated here – although I will examine the issue in section 2.2 (especially footnote 30) – that because the sciences are ideologically biased in the way I indicate, it does not follow that there can be no such thing as 'objectivity' in these sciences.

Appendix

There is developing today another metatheory of social science modelled on the philosophy of science associated with the names of Kuhn and Feyerabend, and it seems relevant to discuss how my remarks relate to this metatheory. Because Kuhn explicitly restricts his analysis to a discussion of theories within sciences, whereas Feyerabend wishes to speak about 'comprehensive ideologies' of which science itself is an example, I will confine myself to Feyerabend. (Of course, the two ought not to be equated with one another; indeed, the difference I cite between them is itself a symptom of important differences in philosophical interests and positions; on this, cf. Feyerabend, 'Consolations for the Specialist' in Lakatos and Musgrave, *Criticism and the Growth of Knowledge*.)

Perhaps the most important point for my purposes is that Feyerabend believes that there is an ideological ingredient in any large-scale theory or basic paradigm; indeed, in his most recent work, 'Against Method', he approvingly quotes Fichte's remark that 'the choice between comprehensive theories rests on one's interests entirely' (p. 128). It is because of this that Feyerabend urges that 'the connection between theory and politics must always be considered' (p. 109). It is in this spirit that he himself discusses the effects of a positivist metatheory of science and epistemology on human communication, as well as focusing attention on the social importance of the principle of proliferation which derives from his 'anarchist epistemology'.

It is on the basis of these specific features, as well as on the general argument of his theory of knowledge, that I think it is fair to say that a follower of Kuhn or Feyerabend would never call for the development of a policy science in the way a positivist would (and which I present in section 2.1), i.e. he would never equate such a development with objective truth coming to rationalise human affairs. On the other hand, the argument which I present in section 2.2, in which I seek to show that there is a conceptual connection between an instrumentalist account of how knowledge is related to action and a certain view, characteristic of modern science, of what knowledge consists of, is precisely in the spirit of Feyerabend's admonitions. For what I am doing in that section is attempting to describe and analyse *the political commitments of the global paradigm which, among other things, seeks to give an explanatory account of events in terms of a distinctive, nomological understanding of cause and effect*. For both Kuhn and Feyerabend believe with the positivists that science gives us causal explanations of a certain type (though they of course differ with the positivists in how they relate such explanations to general theories, how they think the meanings of the terms used in such explanations are determined, how the worth of possible explanations is tested or rival explanations chosen, and so on). In other words, I am articulating certain values implicit in the scientific enterprise itself, values which Feyerabend and others admit are there, but towards which they have not directed their attention.

From the point of view of either a positivist account of science or one amenable to Feyerabend's considerations therefore, it is still possible for me to claim that there are political implications involved in adopting a certain model of social science which is rooted in a certain theory of explanation, though how these two would characterise the acquisition of scientific knowledge and the consequent emergence of a policy science would be dramatically different. What I argue in section 2.2, then, is applicable to both a positivist and a Feyerabendian account of social science.

2

Positivist Social Science and Technological Politics

2.1 *The role of social science in modern political life*

What I write in this section ought to be quite familiar, for the general view I will give is not only to be found in the early development of mainstream social science, but has become one of the mainstays which supports the whole enterprise of social science in our own time. The general view which I propose to give is one that can be culled from the writings of Saint-Simon, Comte, Mill, Weber, and Durkheim, as well as such modern thinkers as Lasswell, Mannheim, Skinner, Lundberg, Robert Lynd, etc.[1] Of course, these writers did not simply repeat each other over the years – indeed, subtle and important distinctions have been made by each of them; consequently, the general view I will present will not do full justice to any one of these thinkers in particular. Nevertheless, what has become a contemporary cliché is rooted in their writings, and what I say will be compatible with their major ideas.

One might begin by asking the question, why have social science at all? Now there are several answers which might be given to this question, but there is one which is strikingly predominant in the writings of social scientists themselves when they reflect on their own work;[2] it is an answer that invokes the

[1] Cf. the Appendix at the end of this chapter for specific references and remarks on this matter.

[2] Here I concentrate on the ideas within the tradition of social science; it would be possible in a larger book to discuss similar ideas found outside of this tradition. For a deep and enlightening analysis of modern political theory in just these terms, cf. S. Wolin, *Politics and Vision*, Chapter 10.

analogy with the natural sciences. For, it is claimed, just as the natural sciences have provided men with a certain kind of knowledge by which they can control their natural environment, thereby making it more hospitable and productive, so also the knowledge gained from social science will enable men to control their social environment, thereby making it more harmonious and congruent with the needs and wants of its members. Natural science gives to men an enormous power based on a knowledge of the workings of the external world, and it is this power which sustains and supports the entire undertaking; so also social science will permit men to control and order the social arrangements which structure their own lives.

In fact, the need for a social science is actually perceived as far more urgent a task than I have so far made it out to be. For many social scientists would claim that it is not merely *desirable* that man's knowledge of his social world become scientific, it is *vital* that this transformation occur. For my purposes one of the most interesting reasons why this should be thought to be so has to do with the rise of industrial society. In the *Division of Labour in Society* Durkheim says that man can escape nature not merely by controlling it but also by creating another world where he himself is at home and secure; this 'world' is society. Underlying this observation is the perception that modern industrial society – which is itself partly engendered by the revolution in thinking and technique caused by the science of nature – is a society so dynamic, divisive, impersonal, and unstable that it cannot be properly governed by any of the traditional political methods. A recurring theme in the social scientific tradition is the necessity for the discovery and implementation of a social structure which is rationally organised so that it can cope with the displacement, the conflicts of interest and need, the rapid change in the forms of social organisation and individual private fortune that characterise a technological society. Therefore, it is argued, because of the social effects of mastering nature through science, technology, and industrial production, society itself must be mastered if social life is going to continue in an uninterrupted and unchaotic way.

Of course this is only part of the story. For another factor that must be taken into account – it was so most articulately by Comte – is that men's attitudes themselves change as a result of the spread of the conceptual assumptions inherent in natural science. For obvious reasons these changes make obsolete or ineffective the religion or magic or traditional justifications from authority which in pre-industrial societies had promoted order, established status, set communal goals, and legitimated authority. Science deprives men of the old faith by which they lived and thus helps to destroy their old social order; thus it can cause suffering and a sense of helplessness in the face of this suffering. It is for this reason that a new faith, one compatible with and arising out of the scientific spirit, must emerge from this chaos and lead men out of the void into which they had been thrown. Social science has a great weight to bear.[3]

I will return to the connection between social science and industrial society at the end of the chapter, for enough has been said to indicate the sorts of concerns which support the efforts to analyse society scientifically. But why, we might ask, does this require a social *science*, conceived as the study of social institutions and social actions with essentially the same epistemology and methodology as employed in the natural sciences? The answer to this is twofold. In the first place, it is claimed, only a scientific study can give us the truly *objective* knowledge of how events or properties of systems are related, and thus it alone can provide us with the power requisite for the task of social control. Older, more traditional attempts at understanding society, particularly those found in political philosophy, are inferior because they mingled among their factual observations mere opinion, because they expressed subjective dispositions and preferences, and because they judged other theories in terms of some vague and unprovable conception of human needs and wants. One can grasp the laws which govern the world – social as well as natural – only if one throws off these adolescent habits of interpreting the world in terms of one's own needs and values, and adopts the mature stance of neutrality *vis-à-vis* one's social world, studying its workings as they are and not how one wishes them to be or how one thinks they ought to be. Only then will the mechanisms which determine this social world reveal themselves as they are.

[3] I think that it was this sort of weight which was partially responsible for the intimate connection between social science and religion in the nineteenth century, to be found, e.g., in Saint-Simonianism, Comte's positivistic religion, and the conclusions reached by Durkheim in *The Elementary Forms of Religious Life*.

It is science, and only science, which adopts this stance, and it does so because it only employs concepts which are rooted in intersubjectively evident observations, because it employs techniques of experimentation which are reproducible, because it utilises reasoning processes which are rigorous and uniformly applicable, and because it accepts explanations only when they predict outcomes which are publicly verifiable.

But the usefulness of science lies not only in the fact that it provides an objectively true account of how the world functions, but also in the sort of account that it gives. Scientific investigations give us causal laws of the type, if C then E under situation X, in which C, E, and X are variables which are specified in terms of observational properties or in terms of some relation to observational properties. Moreover, science fits these causal laws into a deductive chain of wider and wider generality, so that a system of causal laws is formed wherein widely divergent variables are related to one another in a clearly specified and definite way. It is through such systems that one begins to grasp how apparently unrelated phenomena are intimately connected, such that through the manipulation of one variable a whole host of predictable outcomes will occur. It is this ability to predict results that is the basis of the power which scientific knowledge gives to men.

Only a social *science* will give an intersubjectively verifiable (or at least falsifiable) account of how the social world operates, and only a social science will give us causal explanations which are of the type that allow one to prevent the occurrence of an unwanted event, or permit one to bring about the occurrence of one that is desired: it is for this reason that only a social science, conceived as a body of knowledge analogous to that of the natural sciences, can satisfy the condition which modern society demands be satisfied if it is to continue without substantial suffering and ultimately without a total breakdown.

Earlier I mentioned the felt inadequacy of 'traditional political methods', and it seems appropriate at this point to translate what I have been saying into purely political terms, for it is in the political realm that the power promised by social science will be exercised. What sorts of political changes are suggested by such a promise? One might divide these changes into two areas: those dealing with the nature of political argument, and those dealing with institutional changes, specifically the rise of the policy scientist.

In the first place, it is thought that if it were to be the case that political decisions would be made on the basis of technical application of social scientific knowledge, then the character of political argument would drastically alter. The point here is that, at least in the ideal,[4] the disagreements which arise in engineering or medicine are not expressed in terms of personal values or wishes, nor are they debated on the basis of the power or position which the disputants have in the social order to which they belong, nor settled in terms of subtlety of exposition or rhetorical power; rather, the issues are tangible, measurable, and testable, and debates about them are conducted in such a way that it is these objective features accessible to all which decide the matter at hand. In technical arguments one expects to reach mutually acceptable answers, and the reason for this is that it is assumed in such arguments that, given the publicly known parameters of the case, there is one best way to maximise whatever value is to be maximised. If politics were to become an applied science, it is argued, its conjectual, arbitrary, emotional and personal elements would drop out, and its arguments and decisions would assume the same neutral characteristics as those of engineering.

Of course, there are limits to the changes in political decision-making that are possible. In the first place, it does not follow from the argument I have been recounting that no political arguments would be left to divide men; arguments occur in engineering all the time. The point is rather that it is believed there would no longer be arguments as to the kinds of considerations that will

[4] Someone might claim, especially if he were familiar with the literature of the sociology of science, that the advocate of a policy science was being naive here. However, the proponent of this political theory might well respond to this that he is attempting to set out the logic of the situation, what is *in theory* the case, even though he is quite well aware that social factors play a role in scientific arguments. This is necessary in order to bring out clearly and forcefully the differences *in principle* between science and politics, differences which do serve to structure the situations in which politicians and scientists find themselves. In acting in this manner the policy scientist could claim to be following Popper, who distinguishes between the 'third world', where knowledge is developed and changed in a rational manner, and the socio-psychological world where rules are broken and consequently error abounds. A policy science will, at minimum, establish standards of what is correct and what is not, and it is this feature which is being pointed out here.

be admitted as relevant to rational discussion, and, furthermore, that the criteria for truth would be explicitly accepted so that one would be able to determine clearly when they are satisfied, thereby eliciting automatic agreement and permitting conclusions to be transmitted to anyone trained to understand. In political arguments there would be, as there are in scientific arguments, reliable public standards of ascertainable truth, and therefore the possibility of a universally recognisable decisive solution to a particular problem. It is in this way that a social science would be able to eliminate the 'anarchy of opinion' which characterises modern political thinking.

Moreover, it is no longer envisioned that *all* political questions could be translated into, and dealt with, in these technical terms; ever since J. S. Mill[5] everyone has recognised it as necessary to discriminate between 'ends' and 'means' and to relate this to the distinction between 'facts' and 'values'. For once one draws the distinction between 'what is' and 'what ought to be', and one realises that science is only concerned to tell us 'what is the case', it becomes immediately apparent that science cannot tell us what goals we ought to pursue, what direction policy ought to take, what values ought to be promoted. Thus, the policy scientist could not decide the ends which his society ought to seek. Now this might lead someone to think that therefore the idea of a policy scientist is an incoherent one, but, it is argued, this is not the case. In fact, even the engineer doesn't decide what projects ought to be undertaken, but only the best way to accomplish them once such a decision has been made; and even the doctor has to accept the goal of health in order to make his decisions about drugs, operations, and therapy. So also with the policy scientist, for even though he could not tell us the ends we ought to pursue, he could tell us the most efficient *means* to the achievement of these ends. He could do this, just as the engineer and doctor can, because questions of means are resolvable into questions of fact, for they involve the aggregation of benefits and costs defined in terms of some set goal, and these variables can be measured on the basis of a scientific understanding of the social order. Questions about the best means could only be decided if one knew the outcomes of the various alternative

[5] J. S. Mill, *A System of Logic*, Book 5 ch. 12.

courses of action, and it is precisely the causal laws generated by social science which will tell us these outcomes. Instrumental questions are essentially technical in character, and if those in political authority were to utilise the knowledge provided by social science such questions would be objectively solvable.

Thus it is true that the distinction between means and ends does deflate somewhat the importance of the policy scientist, for there is a whole class of important political questions with which he cannot deal; the policy scientist cannot be the saviour of industrial society in quite the way that Saint-Simon, Comte, or Lester Ward had hoped. Nevertheless, one ought not to minimise his role. For, in the first place, it is apparent that the area amenable to scientific judgement is increasing as technical intelligence and problem solving devices become more sophisticated and gradually become applied to areas previously reserved for intuitive judgements based on 'experience'. Moreover, many social scientists[6] argue that the ends of politics are more or less universally accepted and more or less determined by the nature of industrial society anyway, and that it is therefore the means to these accepted ends which are the prime source of disagreement and disruption in technological society. This latter point, it is argued, is related to the spread of the 'scientific attitude' that I mentioned earlier; for once men learn the true nature of their society from social science it seems likely that they would cease to demand ends which are not satisfiable because of the nature of things, and that they would cease to yearn after mutually exclusive ends as well. A 'wise resignation', to use Comte's phrase, characterises the man imbued with the method and knowledge of science. For these reasons the policy scientist will still function as a pivotal figure in the new politics of the future.

There is another distinction that must be introduced at this point, and that is between what Karl Popper calls the 'Piecemeal

[6] This is certainly the case with Saint-Simon. In our own time, this same viewpoint was expressed by all those espousing the 'End of Ideology' (cf. E. Shils, 'The End of Ideology?', *Encounter*, Nov. 1955; S. M. Lipset, *Political Man*, ch. 13; D. Bell, *The End of Ideology*). For other social scientists of the same general view, cf. R. Aron, *Eighteen Lectures on Industrial Society*; J. K. Galbraith, *The New Industrial State*. For a good overview of this whole topic, cf. P. H. Partridge, 'Philosophy, Politics, Ideology' in A. Quinton (ed.), *Political Philosophy*.

Social Engineer' and the 'Historicist Planner'[7]; this is really the difference between attempting to control a specific variable or set of variables within a social system and trying to control the historical development of this system itself. Historicists are those who believe that there are empirical laws of historical development, and that it is the function of social science to make unconditional predictions about the social development of an entire society or even of mankind as a whole; they consequently assign to the planner (or the revolutionary leadership, if that is the case) the task of ushering in the next phase of historical development usually with the idea of 'lessening the birthpangs' associated with this phase.[8] Most social scientists would agree with Popper that historicism rests on a mistake: for the social sciences, as indeed all the sciences, can provide only conditional laws, and these conditional laws can only be used for unconditional predictions when the conditions in question can be taken as given; it is for this reason that long term unconditional predictions are possible only if the systems to which they apply are well isolated, stationary and recurrent (as is the solar system, for example). Now these are not features of social orders, for they are inevitably changing as a result of their dependence on natural phenomena, their interactions with other social systems, and the growth of knowledge and changes in ideas and values of their constituent members. Thus, it is argued, it is a mistake based on a misunderstanding of the nature of science to search for so called laws of history, and it is therefore wrong to conceive of social science as

[7] Cf. Karl Popper, *The Poverty of Historicism*, and 'Predictions and Prophecy in the Social Sciences', *Conjectures and Refutations*, pp. 336–46.

[8] This is the way Marx has most often been interpreted, so that as far as my argument is concerned Marx may be understood as a special sort of positivist whose views on the relation between theory and practice are that social theories provide the laws which the Communist Party applies to concrete social orders, thereby ending the era of human pre-history. Popper himself is partially responsible for this, what I take to be, fundamental misunderstanding of Marx (cf. *The Open Society and Its Enemies*, vol. 2), but it is a deeply rooted misunderstanding that derives from Lenin and ultimately Engels. For another view of Marx in sympathy with the orientation presented in section 3.3 of this book and with the views on theory and practice presented in Chapter 5, cf. S. Avineri, *The Social and Political Thought of Karl Marx*. For an attempt at showing why Marx might be interpreted positivistically, cf. Albrecht Wellmer, *Critical Theory of Society*, ch. 2, 'The Latent Positivism of Marx's Philosophy of History', and Jürgen Habermas, *Knowledge and Human Interests*, ch. 3.

laying the foundation for a policy science which would give complete control over the direction of an entire society's future. Instead, the policy scientist must resign himself to dealing with specific questions about institutions within the framework set by his society.

Thus, there are definite, recognised limits to any policy science. Nevertheless, what is crucial is that in a very large area of political life – that in which instrumental questions are at issue – arguments would still become separated from the personal preferences, the idiosyncratic interests and subjective values of the arguers. The course of the debate would no longer be arbitrary, contingent on personal characteristics and extraneous factors; instead, it would become impersonal and objective, dictated by previously agreed upon considerations as to what is relevant.

This leads naturally to the second political change which would result from the injection of social science into political life, the rise of the policy scientist. I say 'naturally' because only those who have the requisite intelligence and training could possibly engage in the technical argumentation that would comprise political debate if such debate were to take the form I have just outlined. Political leadership would consequently pass, at least in those areas concerned with instrumental questions, to those whose competence enabled them to settle impartially questions of general social interest. Political leadership would become meritocratic, as is scientific leadership, and industrial society would be governed to a large extent by a scientifically knowledgeable elite.

Moreover, the accountability of these experts would be far different from the sort of accountability envisioned in democratic theory, for example. For it would simply not be possible for non-scientists to determine the worth of the policy scientist's decision, just as it is inconceivable that non-engineers could participate in decisions as to how best to construct a bridge or programme the directional rockets on a spaceship. Not only would decisions be made by qualified experts, but these decisions would be immune to attack from the public at large, quite simply because of the public's ignorance.

This emergence of a core of policy scientists would also support the rise of an active and centralised government. For, after all, the utility of social science is that it can direct and guide man's social arrangements towards his own good. Man must engineer his own institutions according to scientifically accurate canons; he must free himself from the unconscious, willy-nilly determination of his future by unknown forces; he must organise his resources to his own design. In short, man must plan, and the function of the social sciences is to provide the theoretical foundation that makes this planning possible. It is this sort of thinking that is in the background which supports the rise of the policy scientists in the first place, and thus it is that if they actually were to emerge it is only natural that their skills would be fully employed.

All through this exposition I have been speaking in the subjunctive mood because the ideas I have been putting forth are largely promissory. But one ought not to conclude that they are therefore not germane to the political affairs of our own day. Obviously, many of the changes that I have suggested are already occurring all around us: today it is plain to everyone that the central government has grown in importance; that technical decisions play an increasingly large part of our political life; that the experts claim an irrefragability for their recommendations based on their assertions that untrained men are incapable of judging their worth; and that the majority opinion is that it is only through increased planning that our pressing social and political problems can be solved. Now it would be utterly fantastic to claim that the doctrine I have been espousing is responsible for these changes – there are obviously socio-economic factors here which are of overwhelming importance. But what is true is that how one regards these changes, how one assesses responsibility, whom one desires to make political decisions, how one argues against specific decisions, how these sorts of issues are settled is a direct function of one's beliefs about the doctrine of a policy science.

What ought to be clear by now is that all of the political changes that I have enumerated are united by an underlying theme which one might call, the sublimation of politics.[9] For what these political changes amount to is an attempt to eliminate politics as we know it, overcoming its limitations and uncertainties by replacing it with a form of social engineering analogous to the applied physical sciences. The view I have presented seeks to destroy the claim – inherent in any sort of democratic theory of

[9] Cf. S. Wolin, *Politics and Vision*, ch. 10.

government – that political argument can be settled only in terms of the value-ascribing discourse of political philosophy and traditional political action, a claim which is based on the assumption that in politics any proposal incorporates the values of its proponents, and that in the last analysis there are value stances which are incompatible and irreconcilable. To the policy scientist this is the worst sort of irrationalism; for him, objective answers established through the rational use of evidence and technique will replace opinion and rhetoric and persuasion, and social life will be thereby redeemed from the uninformed guesses and purely subjective life-preferences of politicians and thus transformed into a rational enterprise.

Implicit in this belief that an applied science can perform the tasks now seen as political is the tacit presumption that science provides the paradigm example of proper thinking, and that as long as any human enterprise is not treated in a scientific way it is being treated in an imperfect way.[10] It is this viewpoint which underlies the single most important element in the whole social engineering view of politics, which is that there is a *correct* way of proceeding in human affairs and that it is the responsibility of the decision-maker to discover what this way is. As in the building of a bridge or the repairing of a broken arm, so also in social affairs there is a right mode of operation which is inherent in the matter at hand and in the nature of the problem. Until now the unreliable intuitions and the muddled impressions 'based on experience' of the politicians have prevented men from going about finding the rational way to proceed, but the methods of science will overcome this disastrous manner of deciding what to do. At least with respect to instrumental questions, a policy science will be able to do clearly and accurately what politics has been fumblingly trying to accomplish all along; and with the maturation of such a science, truth, transcending the ignorance, the pettiness, and the self-interestedness of political men will finally prevail in the authoritative decisions which determine the way in which resources and values are allocated in a society.

Social science is indeed critical for politics. It will change the

[10] One might compare here Plato's belief in the identification of philosophy with the rational, and his consequent desire to make politics philosophical. The desire to eliminate politics has a history deeply embedded in human thought.

nature of much, if not all, of political argument, making it technical and therefore soluble; it will press the scientific expert to the fore, at last establishing authority on the grounds of competence and expertise rather than on the quite arbitrary and manifestly unsatisfactory basis of heredity, wealth, social status, or demagogic power. Thus, much of political life will be transformed into a rational activity in which policy is made on explicit, objective, impartial criteria of efficiency; in Saint-Simon's now famous phrase, government, in the sense of government of men by men, will be abolished in large measure, and in its place will be inaugurated 'the administration of things'. When this time arrives, a new period of man's history will dawn, for through the manipulative powers gained as a result of social scientific knowledge, and it alone, man will achieve the satisfaction of his desires and consequently the happiness for which he longs. All of this today has become commonplace.

2.2 *The idea of science and the idea of its use: how they are linked*

The above account of the notion of a policy science details a particular theory of the way in which the knowledge gained from social science may be used. At this point a critical commentator might say something like the following: the picture that you have just presented really has nothing to do with the nature of social science in itself, but is only one of the many possible ways that one might conceptualise the use to which the knowledge gained from this science might be put. In other words, you have given us a *political theory* which, while dependent upon the existence of a social science positivistically conceived, is only contingently related to the idea of such a science. A person holding this view of social science *need not* hold this view of its political relevance – he may or he may not, but whatever he decides is logically independent of his views regarding the nature of social science.

In response to this one might well wish to begin by pointing out that this is surely not historically accurate. Anyone who examines the genesis of the idea of a positivist science of social institutions and behaviour in the late eighteenth and nineteenth centuries, and who follows the developments in this idea up to our own time, is immediately struck by the political self-consciousness in light of which many of the best and most important theorists in this tradition constructed their ideas.[11] Indeed, it would not be an exaggeration to say that often it was the political ideal which determined what a particular writer said about the nature of social science, and that this was certainly true when the basic canons of description and explanation, which became the fundamental assumptions of all the subsequent writings on these questions, were being hammered out.[12]

Still, the reply might run, this in itself does not establish a *conceptual* link between a positivist conception of social science and the notion of a policy science. The connection between them may be a historical accident, or, perhaps more believably, it may be that only certain sorts of people committed to a certain political persuasion became interested and involved in social science; in either case the particular political beliefs did not determine what the conception of social science was. Indeed, one could also point to the fact that the positivist conception of social science did not invariably produce engineering-type political beliefs; even in the nineteenth century there were social scientists of high repute – Herbert Spencer and the neo-classical economists, for example – who held to a *laissez-faire* theory of government, and indeed who thought that their scientific findings would lend support to this political theory. And, of course, there are many social scientists today whose metatheory of social science is positivist and yet whose political theory is far from that of the policy scientist.

It is at this point that one must face directly the issue of whether there is in fact a conceptual connection[13] between a view of how one ought to understand social life and a view of how this understanding is to be translated into action. Is there such a connection between a positivist *theory* of social knowledge and a social engineering conception of political *practice*? I think that there is, and that this can be demonstrated by examining, first, the conception of explanation which is at the heart of the positivist theory of science, and second, the conceptual assumptions which underlie the whole scientific enterprise, assumptions

[11] Cf. the list of works cited in the Appendix at the end of this chapter.

[12] I have in mind here Mill, Durkheim, and Weber, as well as the more obvious candidates, Comte and Saint-Simon.

[13] What is meant by a 'conceptual connection' will become clearer as the argument develops, especially p. 38 ff.

which themselves account for the theory of explanation within science. When I have finished making these essentially philosophical arguments, I then want to go on to make a few brief remarks, in the tradition of Max Weber, about the interconnections between science, rationalisation, control, and industrial society; I do this with the idea of setting the more philosophical remarks within a larger sociological framework, and thereby investing them with more historical significance.

In order to show the conceptual connection between science and control, a connection which is at the heart of my claim that a certain conception of social science implicitly contains a notion of how theory is related to practice, I must first demonstrate the interrelationship between scientific explanation and prediction; it is only then that I will be able to show that the possibility of control is a constitutive element in the scientific enterprise itself. I will start with a straightforward and oft repeated account of the structural identity of scientific explanation and prediction, and then go on to examine several objections that have been raised against this view.

Say that E is a state of affairs that the scientist wants to explain; how does he accomplish this task? It is generally said that he does so when he is able to indicate the determining factors or causes which produce E.[14] Now discovering the causes of E is discovering those features of the situation which, taken together, invariably result in E; it is this notion of invariability which is crucial in an explanation, for we can say that we have

[14] Following Nagel (*Structure of Science*, ch. 2) one could also claim that the sciences provide genetic, functional, or probabilistic explanations. But genetic explanations are really only stories based on the conjunction of a number of causal factors arranged in a certain way, and are thus only a special case of the kind I am discussing here. Related to genetic explanations is the so-called 'intelligibility theory of explanation' which claims that scientific explanations are ones in which certain models which underlie a range of processes are explicated; these models, however, incorporate causal processes, so that, while identifying causal factors is not sufficient for an explanation to be complete, according to this theory, it is a necessary feature. With regard to functional explanations, while it is a highly debatable point whether they are of the same logical type as causal explanations, they do rest on causal explanations; moreover, it is also the case that scientists seek to replace functional accounts with causal ones as explanations of a far more satisfactory sort. I will examine probabilistic explanations in a moment. It should also be noted that everything that I say about explanation could just as well be expressed in the language of functions.

explained E only when we can see that E had to happen given certain explanatory facts, which means to say that it is an instance of some general regularity of nature. Once we see this we understand that what once appeared as a puzzling event is not now puzzling at all.

The logical form of this type of explanation is the well known deductive-nomological (D-N) model of explanation. It consists of relating the statement describing E to a series of statements about other states of affairs C . . . C_N and to one or more general laws L_N, such that the statement of E (the explanandum) is logically deducible from the statement of C_N (the initial conditions) and the general law(s); the upshot of this is that, given the explanation, the E state of affairs could not have been other than it was – we see why it *had* to be, and thus we have explained it. This particular model is one form of what is called the covering law model of explanation; it is also identified in this manner in order to draw attention to the central importance of the general law in scientific explanation. The deduction from the statement about the initial conditions to the statement of the explanandum event is possible only because of the presence of this universal, well confirmed empirical hypothesis of conditional form which states that under certain specified boundary conditions every case in which the states of affairs of the type C_N occur a state of affairs of the type E will also occur.

It might be difficult at this point to see how the D-N model of explanation is indeed a model of causal explanation. Actually, causal explanations are the most important type of deductive-nomological explanation,[15] for most frequently the general laws employed in the D-N model are causal laws and therefore the initial conditions are said to be causes of the explanandum event. In causal laws the relationship between the variables mentioned in the law must satisfy three conditions: the relationship must be invariable; one variable must temporally precede, or at least be simultaneous with, the other; and the relationship must be asym-

[15] Other types of D-N explanation which fit the D-N model are, for example, those which employ laws of co-existence, such as Boyle's Law, in the explanation of a certain phenomenon; or those which employ laws of natural kinds, which assert a specified set of properties in every object of a certain kind, in an explanation of the properties of a given system or object. The point regarding these other types of explanation is, however, that science continually tries to incorporate them into a system of causal or functional laws.

metrical, such that the occurrence of one (the independent) variable induces the occurrence of the other (dependent) variable, while the reverse is not true. Causal laws, therefore, state an invariable sequential order of dependence between kinds of states of affairs.

D-N forms of explanation of the causal variety can quite easily be reformulated into the language of necessary and sufficient conditions, which is the way that causality has most often been presented since J. S. Mill, and which is the way most social scientists are familiar with it. When someone asserts that X causes Y, what he is asserting is that X is of the type A and Y is of the type B, and that A and B are related in such a way that whenever A occurs B occurs (such that A is a sufficient condition of B), or that without A, B could not have occurred (such that A is a necessary condition of B), or a combination of these two statements. I made X and Y instances of types A or B in order to indicate the generality involved in causal claims, for once this implied generality is grasped the relationship between a D-N analysis of causality and one formulated in terms of necessary and sufficient conditions becomes quite clear. For any claim that X causes Y in the sense that X is a necessary and/or a sufficient condition of Y involves the assumption of a general law to the effect that *whenever* X occurs Y will occur, or that *whenever* X does not occur Y will not occur, or both and this is to say that any ascription of causality involves reference not only to the initial conditions, in this case X, but these together with the general law which asserts an invariable, functional relationship between a dependent and an independent variable.

Once it is seen that causal explanations can be expressed in terms of the D-N model, what has been called the 'structural identity' of explanation and prediction ought to be apparent; for the terms of a prediction and an explanation, as well as the relations between them, are similar. In the case of a prediction the statements of the relevant general laws and the particular facts are given and the statement describing a particular event not yet known to have occurred is deduced from them; in the latter case, the event is known to have occurred, and the general laws and statements about particular facts from which it can be deduced are sought. A prediction is thus simply the obverse of a causal explanation. This of course does not mean that the two are the same thing; they differ from one another with respect to the theorist's information, explanation dealing with events that are known to have occurred, prediction with events not known to have occurred.

In light of the structural identity of explanation in science and prediction it may be said – and this is the most important point for my purposes – *that an explanation is not complete unless it could have functioned as a prediction.*[16] For if the explanandum state of affairs can be derived from the initial conditions and the general laws stated in the explanation, then it might have been predicted before it actually happened on the basis of the knowledge provided in the explanation. The very condition of explanation is its logical structure which makes prediction possible.[17]

It is important to note that the claim is that every adequate explanation in science is *potentially* a prediction, for failure to pay sufficient attention to this formulation gives rise to the first of the three objections I wish to consider to the view that in science explanations and predictions are logically homomorphic. The objection[18] is that at any given time the information that would be required if one were to make a predictive use of a particular law might not be available, even though such a law is explanatory of a given event, because the requisite information is only available *ex post facto,* and it is therefore the case that explanatory power and predictive power are not the same thing. (An example of this[19] is the usefulness of the concept 'fitness' in evolutionary theory in *explaining* the survival of a certain species even though it is not at present possible to have *predicted* on the basis of this information that the species would have survived, and this is because the conditions mentioned in the covering law are at present unpredictable.) But this objection is mistaken. For scientific explanations are conditional in form, which is to say that they assume that both the initial conditions and the boundary conditions are as the explanans says they are, so that in

[16] This does not imply the reverse, that every adequate predicition is potentially an explanation.

[17] It is in terms of this crucial feature of explanation that one must understand the importance of experimental predictions as tests of theories in science.

[18] Cf. S. Morgenbesser, 'Is it a Science?', in A. MacIntyre and D. Emmett, *Sociological Theory and Philosophical Analysis.*

[19] Cf. M. Scriven, 'Explanation and Prediction in Evolutionary Theory', *Science,* 130, 1959.

explaining the explanandum state of affairs one does not *also* have to explain (or predict) the occurrence of these conditions. Another way of saying this is that all scientific explanations *presuppose* a closed system within which the operations of the various factors are as the explanation says they are, so that such explanations do not explain the existence or character of this system – that would require another explanation. But how are these explanations explanatory then? They are so because they allow one to claim that he *could* have predicted the occurrence of the event *if* he had been able to have all the relevant information at hand; the fact that in some cases one cannot predict when and if the states of affairs which comprise this relevant information will be forthcoming does not mean that one therefore has explained an event even though one could not have predicted it, for both one's explanations and one's predictions *assume* that these certain states of affairs exist. Thus, the structural identity of explanation and prediction is still maintained, such that by explaining the occurrence of an event in terms of certain conditions one is thereby laying the foundation for predicting this event in terms of these very same conditions. Whether one can explain/predict the occurrence of *these* conditions is another matter.

Another possible objection[20] comes from the assertion that a scientific explanation may only explain how a certain state of affairs was possible by providing the necessary conditions for its occurrence ('without X, no Y'),[21] and in this case the law does not provide the requisite information for predicting new occurrences of the explanandum. So in these instances at least, it is claimed, it is a mistake to think that a causal explanation is equivalent to a mechanism for predicting the phenomenon explained.

Apart from the question of whether this sort of explanation by itself constitutes an adequate explanation,[22] this objection can

[20] Cf. ibid, p. 480.

[21] Scriven's formulation is 'the only cause of Y is X' which is to say *at least* that 'without an X there is no Y'. May Brodbeck has argued, correctly I believe, that there is something more implied here as well in order for this to figure in an explanation, and that it is this extra ingredient which vitiates Scriven's argument; however, I want to deal with the 'necessary condition argument' directly. Cf. M. Brodbeck, *Minnesota Studies*, vol. 3.

[22] Cf. the Brodbeck article cited in the footnote above.

be met on its own terms by demonstrating that such explanations are predictive in an indirect sense. For if we know the necessary conditions of an event we thereby know that by insuring their absence we will thereby insure the absence of the event, i.e. we can predict that it will *not* occur. It is in this way that a certain sort of causal law can be used to prevent the occurrence of an event, rather than, as in the ordinary case, to bring it about. The important point here is that, *in just the same way that one explains the event,* one is thereby able to make predictions about it, for in both cases one is working in terms of the factors which make the occurrence or non-occurrence of the event a *possibility.*

There is a third objection[23] to the thesis which I have presented which is of acute importance for the social sciences, and this has to do with the fact that in science there is another form of explanation, called the inductive-probabilistic (I-P) model, which does not employ laws of the type I have been discussing, but rather uses laws of statistical probability. Statistical laws state that under certain conditions which constitute the performance of a random experiment, a certain kind of outcome will occur in a specified (usually very high) percentage of cases. Because the laws involved in this type of explanation are of this form, the relationship between the explanans (the general laws and the statement of the initial conditions) and the statement of the explanandum cannot be a deductive one; instead it is one of inductive support in which the 'premises' of the argument make more or less likely the 'conclusion' of the argument, to the effect that the event occurred. Now this is significant for the issue of the structural identity of explanation and prediction, for, as can be seen, it is in the very nature of this sort of explanation that it admits the possibility that E might have failed to occur, so that it does *not* allow one to predict that, given the conditions mentioned in the explanation, E will occur. So here there seems to be a wedge between explanation and prediction.

There are several possible answers to this. In the first place, it is a question whether inductive-probabilistic explanations actually do explain the occurrence of a single event E, for given an explanation of such an event in these terms one still wants to ask, why on this particular occasion did E not fail to occur as it might

[23] Cf. N. Hanson, 'On the Symmetry between Explanation and Prediction', *The Philosophical Review*, 68, 1959.

have according to the explanation? (An alternative conception of the inductive-probabilistic model with respect to single events might be, therefore, that it does not offer an explanation of the occurrence of the event, but that it rather provides evidence which justifies *our expecting* E to occur). Be this as it may, it certainly is the case that in so far as one claims to have explained E in this way one does so by showing that E was a highly probable outcome, which means to say that one could have predicted its occurrence with a very high degree of probability. What is important here is that while the prediction of the event is probabilistic, so also is the explanation of the event, so that the structural identity of the two is maintained. Indeed, the I-P model allows one to predict the relative frequency with which a given event will occur, and it is just this ability to predict which enables one to say that one has explained the event.

In the second place, I-P explanations are often used to explain mass-events rather than individual events. Thus, one may use a statistical law to explain why it is that X per cent of the atoms in a milligram of uranium have decayed over a certain period of time, although one could not use this law to explain why *this* atom and not that one decayed. In this case it is clear that the I-P explanation does explain precisely in so far as it provides the rational basis for the prediction of such a mass event.

Thus, even though there are a number of possible objections to the thesis of the structural identity of explanation in science and prediction which require several emendations of the thesis, its basic truth still stands. The question now is, what bearing does this discussion have on the question of the relation of theory to practice? Its relevance is neatly summed up in Comte's epigram, 'From Science comes Prevision, from Prevision comes Control.' For, precisely because scientific explanations are the obverse of predictions, they lay the foundation for the instrumental control of phenomena by providing the sort of information which would enable one to manipulate certain variables in order to bring about a state of affairs or prevent its occurrence.[24] It is thus no accident that social science positivistically conceived is histori-

[24] Or at least it provides information useful in preparing for the inevitable in the case of systems over which we at present have no control, such as the solar system. Indeed, with regards to these systems, one might say that science provides the information for their *possible* technical control.

cally linked with a social engineering viewpoint, for it is in the very nature of the sort of understanding given to us by science that it underlies such a viewpoint.

But, our objector might retort at this point, even though science does provide the information which *would* enable one to control phenomena through technical manipulation, the scientist *need not* relate to particular phenomena in this way: it is up to him to decide whether he wants to use his knowledge in this way, and such a decision would be an extra-scientific one. So, the objector might continue, all the argumentation so far still has not met the principal objection voiced at the beginning of this discussion, namely, that just because there is a historical connection between a positivist conception of social theory and a social engineering conception of how this theory is related to practice, this does not mean that there is a conceptual connection between them. In effect, he might claim, all that has been shown in demonstrating that science lays the basis for manipulative control is why someone with an engineering sort of political theory would turn to the promise of such a social science; surely it has not been shown why this conception of social theory commits one to this sort of political theory.

But the basis upon which this objection rests is false, and an examination of why it is false will enable me to demonstrate not merely that the positivist conception of social science underlies and supports the idea of a policy science – something which has admittedly already been done – but that it is conceptually connected with it. To begin with, it is inaccurate to assert that, in the context of practical decision-making,[25] 'it is up to the individual scientist to decide whether he wants to use his knowledge in this

[25] Of course, because I am discussing the relation of social theory to political practice, I am presupposing this context of practical action. It is possible for someone to refuse to act, and to acquire scientific knowledge for the purpose of aesthetic contemplation; it is for this reason that I am not claiming that a positivist philosophy of social science logically entails an engineering political theory, but only that it implies such a political theory if one is attempting to work out how the knowledge gained from one's theory can be useful for political life. Moreover, such a contemplative attitude would be a schizoid one, for, as I shall show in a moment, it is the possibility of technical control which constitutes the transcendental framework of science in the first place, and it is also this possibility which gives to science its social meaning in an industrial society, so that for both of these reasons to view scientific knowledge as contemplative seems to undermine both the philosophical and sociological point of the enterprise.

way', for, given the form which scientific knowledge takes,[26] there is no other way that such knowledge can be useful in making practical decisions *except in an instrumentalist manner.* Science provides us with objective causal laws in which a certain state of affairs or type of state of affairs is explained by showing how other states of affairs either produce or prevent it; if a man turns to science, therefore, in order to learn how to cope with a state of affairs, the only information that it provides is the means by which, through certain technical operations, he can produce or prevent it, or, in the case of systems over which he has no control, how he can prepare himself in order to mitigate its effects. Scientific explanations give man power to act in situations by giving him the knowledge by which he can control phenomena through the manipulation of a particular set of variables.

Moreover, and much deeper, is the fact that the connection between the form which scientific knowledge takes and an instrumentalist conception of theory and practice lies at the very heart of what the nature of the scientific enterprise is; for, I would argue, the possibility of technical control, far from having a contingent relationship to science, is indeed part of the framework which constitutes the very possibility of scientific activity. I now want to show why this is so.[27]

A good place to begin is with the question, why is it the case that in science to explain something is to potentially predict it? Asking this question forces one immediately to see that the conception of explanation which I elucidated earlier in this chapter rests on a theory of what is to count as understanding an event or state of affairs, namely, that to understand an event or state of

[26] Science also provides us with descriptions of the world, and someone might claim that this is a 'form of knowledge' which does not lead to an instrumentalist conception of how knowledge is related to action. But quite apart from the question of whether mere descriptions apart from their role in scientific explanations of the sort I have been discussing are part of 'scientific knowledge', there is also the question of the relation between the kind of descriptions which science provides on the one hand, and the possibility of technical control which underlies the scientific enterprise as a whole, on the other; I will explore this latter question in a moment.

[27] For an account of the sort of argument that I will now make, cf. G. Radnitzsky, *Contemporary Schools of Metascience*, vol. 2, ch. 1 and vol. 3, ch. 1. He calls this type of analysis the 'philosophical anthropology of knowledge'. For the clearest and simplest account of this, cf. K. O. Apel, 'The *A Priori* of Communication and the Foundation of the Humanities", *Man and World*, vol. 5, no. 1, Feb. 1972. This thesis is discussed briefly in the Preface to the New Edition of Lucien Goldman's *The Human Sciences and Philosophy*.

affairs is to know another event which will invariably produce or prevent it.[28] But this is to say that *we understand a state of affairs scientifically only to the extent that we have the knowledge of what to do in order to control it,*[29] and *it is thus that the ability to control phenomena provides the framework in terms of which scientific explanation proceeds.*

Of course this theory of understanding is itself rooted in a whole series of metaphysical assumptions as to the nature of truth and reality, but this is a topic far beyond the scope of this book.[30] But even at a superficial level it ought to be apparent that for the scientist reality is comprised of observable objects and events which are related nomologically, i.e. they are related according to a series of general laws of the type, if X then Y under situation C, and that therefore, in line with this scientific assumption about reality, only statements which reveal the concrete forms which those general relationships take can be true statements. Science must view the world in this way in order for it to provide the kind of explanations it prizes, which is to say, in order for it to provide the control over the phenomena which is a sign of its having understood a phenomenon. Because science marks out the 'world' as a world of observable phenomena subject to general laws it thereby is *constituting this 'world' from the viewpoint of how one can gain control over it.* It is for this

[28] It is important to remember at this point that there exist alternative conceptual schemes which give different accounts of what it means to understand something. What the concept 'understand' means depends on human conventions; what I am trying to do here is to articulate the presuppositions which underlie the conventions of science. I shall actually discuss an alternative set of conventions by way of contrast in a moment.

[29] Of course, to have this knowledge is one thing, and actually to be able to employ it is another; this is a technical problem which does not affect the issue of what is to count as understanding in science. It is for this reason that what I say applies even to these sciences in which men at present have little opportunity of controlling variables, e.g. astronomy or geology.

[30] One might read, in this regard, Francis Bacon's *Novum Organum*, Book 1 (1620) and his *New Atlantis* (1627). Bacon's overwhelming importance in the development of the positivist conception of social science in the eighteenth and nineteenth centuries is due not only to his (quite misleading) philosophy of science and corresponding methodological strictures, as is usually noted, but even more to his laying bare the metaphysical assumptions which underpin the scientific world view, and especially how they are related to a conception of human needs and interests and to instrumental action. For a full discussion of the interest-grounding of the scientific enterprise, cf. Jurgen Habermas, *Knowledge and Human Interests*, especially ch. 5.

reason that possible technical control provides the framework within which the definition of reality and truth in science occurs.

Underlying and informing the theory of explanation which I have presented are deeper assumptions as to the nature of truth and reality, and these deeper assumptions are rooted in the notion of manipulative control. So the conclusion is not merely that scientific knowledge provides the basis for manipulative control, but also, and more importantly, that what can count as scientific knowledge is that which gives us the means by which one can in principle control phenomena.[31] The possibility of controlling variables is a factor in terms of which one distinguishes a cognitive enterprise as scientific, and thus technical control is a defining element in the scientific enterprise itself.

This might be somewhat clearer if it is contrasted with another conceptual scheme which employs a different notion of truth and therefore of explanation. For there is a long tradition in Western thought which holds that to explain something is to show its final cause, i.e. to demonstrate its purpose in the scheme of things; now this theory of explanation can be found in any number of different conceptual schemes, and the Christian world-view is

[31] It is important to emphasise that what I am saying here is that it is what *can count* as scientific knowledge that is defined by men, and not that what is *true* is simply decided by them. For the *truth* of a theory depends on the state of the world; it is what it *means* for a theory to be true that depends on human conventions.

It is of overwhelming importance to make this distinction between meaning and truth, as well as to distinguish between the related concepts of ethical neutrality and objectivity; for a failure to do so leads one into making such absurd statements as, 'whether some proposition is true or not is a subjective matter, up to the individual person,' or 'because our knowledge is rooted in some ideological conceptions, there is no possibility of an intersubjective validation of a knowledge claim'. These statements are absurd because they do violence to the concept of 'knowledge' and 'truth'. They are made because the person fails to draw the distinctions I just mentioned; and, I would also submit, this failure is itself rooted in the further mistake of failing to differentiate between what can be said about the categories of our thought on the one hand, and about propositions uttered in terms of these categories on the other.

Even though what it means for a proposition to be true is a result of human conventions, and even though these conventions could have been otherwise than they are, and even though they contain ideological components, it does not follow that this proposition cannot be objectively true in an important sense. Thus, men decide what it means to say that 'it is raining outside', but men do not decide, given this meaning, whether this proposition is true, i.e. they do not decide whether it is raining—for *that* they have to look and see.

one of them. For a strictly Christian understanding of even natural events, as well as of human history, is one which views phenomena as episodes in the story of God's relationship with his creation, so that to understand these phenomena is to grasp their meaning in terms of this story, is to see how they fit into the pattern of revelation, consolation, guidance and judgement which are chapters in God's overall plan for mankind. Thus, from this viewpoint the Bible is a document which explains phenomena, though from the scientific world-view it obviously is not explanatory. The point here is that there are alternative notions of what can count as an explanation, and that, in so far as some choice is required,[32] the choice involves some metaphysical conceptions as to the nature of truth and, beyond that, the nature of the world and the place of man in it.[33]

What underlies the scientific conception of explanation is the assumption that to understand an event is to know the events which produced it – and not just any events either, but those natural events which preceded it in time and which invariably produce the event in question. The scientist says that he knows what happened when he knows the causes of the event, and he means by this when he knows the mechanism in terms of which he himself can in theory produce the event in an experimental situation. All of this means that the notion of understanding in

[32] It is possible to argue—and this has frequently been argued since the rise of science—that the Christian need not view a scientific explanation of phenomena as antithetical to his own, but rather as supplementary to it. But my point here is that the two *can indeed be incompatible*, for example, in the case of the intervention of a non-natural force into natural processes (the creation story), and into human history (the punishment for sin being a cause of human suffering).

[33] If the example I offer sounds a bit far-fetched to modern ears, then I suggest that the reader look at Teilhard de Chardin's enormously influential and highly praised, *The Phenomenon of Man*. In this book, Father de Chardin offers an explanation of natural and human evolution in terms of final causes set by God: he claims that we can only understand the world by grasping the 'within the matter' (radial energy) and the yearning of physical matter to reach its completion and 'home', the Omega Point. De Chardin, a noted paleontologist, argues that he is offering a new sort of science, which is to say that he is attempting to convince the readers to change their scientific ideas of what it means to understand phenomena and to adopt a new meaning of the concept 'understanding'. For a scientist's rejoinder which demonstrates the philosophical unacceptability of this account from the point of view of modern science, and which therefore brings out the contrast I am trying to draw, cf. Sir Peter Medawar's 'The Phenomenon of Man' in *The Art of the Soluble.*

science is intimately bound up with the notion of control, for it is our ability to control events, at least in principle, which constitutes one of the criteria in virtue of which one can be said to have given a valid scientific explanation. It is in this way that the possibility of control is a constitutive element of the scientific enterprise, and this means to say that *it is its* (*instrumental*) *conception of the relation of theory to practice that gives the scientific conception of truth its meaning and therefore sets the conditions for the validity of a scientific explanation.* It is just this conclusion which supports my claim that a positivist conception of the knowledge of social life contains within itself an instrumentalist-engineering conception of the relation of this knowledge to social action; for one is committed to this engineering view of theory and practice in the very act of adopting the positivist view of theory – indeed, it is this engineering view which supports and gives meaning to this view of social theory. Thus it is no accident or contingent sociological fact that the notion of a policy science is one that is deeply ingrained in the development of positivistic social science itself; rather, the articulation of this notion and its ramifications is simply a drawing out of the consequences of adopting a certain conception of social theory, consequences which were inherent in this conception all along.

Of course, this is not to say that the essentially manipulative character of scientific knowledge is so because of the *intentions* of individual scientists, such that my claim would be an empirical one that could be falsified by asking scientists whether or not this was their aim in doing their work. Rather, I am making a philosophical claim as to the *meaning* of the scientific enterprise, attempting to illuminate the *a priori* structure of assumptions which constitutes the very possibility of this enterprise, a structure which its pracitioners take for granted and work within, and therefore one which they need not formulate in order to do their work. It is only by being self-conscious about the foundations of what he is doing, i.e. only by being philosophical, that a social scientist would be able to articulate the conceptual linkages between the idea of a policy science and the idea of a positivist theory of social science. But this does not invalidate the claim that there are these linkages, and this is all that I am asserting.

To this point my arguments have been philosophical and

abstract; in order to appreciate their relevance to concrete historical practice, it is necessary to view the conclusions that have been reached in the context of the development of modern industrial society. Of course such a task would be enormous if done fully, but a few remarks will indicate the sorts of considerations that might be brought to bear; here I intend to be merely suggestive.

For this analysis the concept of rationalisation as developed by Max Weber is extremely useful. 'Rationalisation' refers to the process by which growing areas of social life are subjected to decisions made in accordance with technical rules for the choice between alternative strategies given some set of goals or values. The characteristic features of these sorts of decisions are the quantification of the relevant data, the use of formal decision procedures, and the utilisation of empirical laws; all of these are combined to form an attitude of abstraction from the traditional, qualitative, and historically unique features of a situation in order to settle the question at hand 'objectively'. This sort of instrumental rationality is intimately connected with control over the various factors at hand, such that, by the manipulation of certain variables in accordance with some plan, some goal is best achieved. According to Weber the first and most important area of modern social life to become organised along these lines was the economic, in which the processes of production were 'made rational' in order to increase labour productivity and therefore profit.[34]

Now the relevance of this to my discussion of the idea of a positivist social science is simply this: the institutionalisation of science arose in the context of the growing rationalisation of modern life, *and this is precisely because science is linked to the promise of possible technical control.* And it is because of this connection between theory and practice which a positivist view of social theory contains that such a social science gains its cultural significance in modern life. Let me amplify this a bit.

One important cultural support for the scientific enterprise in general lies in its providing the means by which continued expansion of the forces of production can be guaranteed. Now this seems quite clear with respect to the natural sciences, for

[34] On this, cf. Max Weber, 'Sociological Categories of Economic Action', in *The Theory of Social and Economic Organisation*, ed. by T. Parsons, pp 158–320.

through their provision of the appropriate natural knowledge improvements in productive technique and the development of new products occur,[35] but the same observation holds for the social sciences as well, for they promise to provide the sort of information needed to organise and administer the men participating in the processes of production.[36] The reason why this is so is the obvious but important truth that the exploitation of nature for the production of goods and services can only occur through the co-operative effort of men who undertake to do the work involved. This truth becomes a pre-eminent fact in a society which is devoted to a constant increase in production through the self-conscious organisation of social labour; for in these societies rational administration directed towards ensuring continuity of operation, speed, precision, and an efficient employment of men and machines leads to an increasing division of labour in which men come to perform quite specialised functions, and in such a complex economy productive activity can go forward only when this activity is performed according to some highly abstract and general plan. It is in this context of the necessity of rational management that the central importance of bureaucratic planning and bureaucratic forms of organisation in modern life must be understood. Appropriately, the large corporation is a key example of this entire process.[37]

Moreover, an industrial system is an inherently dynamic one, not only because innovation in the means of production is institutionalised, but also because increasing areas of life are brought under the same sort of 'rationality' as characterises the

[35] Actually the utilisation of natural science for technological improvement began to have significance only in the mid-nineteenth century, but it is a fundamental feature of advanced industrial economics. For a discussion of the inter-relationships between natural science, industry and industrial society, cf. P. Rossi, *Philosophy, Technology and the Arts in the Early modern Era*, and A. Musson and E. Robinson, *Science and Technology in the Industrial Revolution*.

[36] For a discussion of the interrelationship of social science and industrial society, cf. J. K. Galbraith, *The New Industrial State;* C. Wright Mills, *The Sociological Imagination*, especially ch. 5, 'The Bureaucratic Ethos'. Raymond Aron, *The Industrial Society*, especially the second essay entitled, 'Development Theory and Evolutionist Philosophy'.

[37] On this, cf. Max Weber, 'Bureaucracy', in *From Max Weber*, eds. Gerth and Mills, pp. 106–264, and 'Legal Authority with a Bureaucratic Administrative Staff' in *The Theory of Social and Economic Organisation*, ed. T. Parsons, pp. 329–40.

economic sphere. In the beginning this rationalisation of spheres of life is extended to those areas which are immediately needed to support the continuation of the production process (so that, from the organisation and utilisation of labour, rationalisation moves outward to include those institutions involved in trade, to the network of transportation and communication, to financial administration, to the school system to supply trained workers, and so on). But as this process continues, another factor, namely the growing status accorded to this type of thinking, begins to assume importance as well, and thus it comes to be employed in dealing with all facets of life.

In this process the nature of political life is, not surprisingly, dramatically affected, and this is most important for my purposes. For while it is historically true that in its initial stages of development industrial society involved a separation of the economic sphere from political control, so that production could develop unhampered by regressive political authorities whose legitimacy survived from pre-industrial times – this, of course, was expressed in the liberal ideologies of the day – in its later stages one can witness a progressively massive increase in state intervention in the economic affairs and social organisation of a country, an intervention which has assumed the forms of welfare statism, the managed economy, and state socialistic planning. This state intervention is due in large part to the inherent instability of the industrial system left to its own devices. The upshot of this is that politics comes to be thought of as an activity primarily directed toward supporting the smooth development of the production processes among various sectors, eliminating dysfunctions which appear in the system as a whole, and enlisting mass support for the system by ensuring a minimum of goods and services for large numbers of the population. In other words, politics comes to be thought of as synonomous with the administration of the industrial system; it becomes itself a form of technical activity, in which political questions are interpreted as essentially technical questions which demand instrumentalist decisions.

It is in this way that the process of rationalisation pushes outward from its original economic base – where the development of natural science seemed most important – so that it finally comes to include politics as well – in which the development of a technically exploitable social science is thought to be an urgent necessity.[38]

It is in light of these sorts of considerations that the technocratic viewpoint I presented in section 2.1 can best be understood. But even more important for the purposes of the argument I have been making, to the effect that a positivist conception of social science contains within itself the idea of technical manipulation, is that these two ideas are linked in the historical process of rationalisation which characterises modern society.[39] In other words, it is *because* of its conceptual connections with the idea of control that a positivist social science has the relevance and institutional backing that it has in modern life.

The philosophical arguments that linked science and the transcendental viewpoint of possible technical control assume social significance when they are embedded in the sociological construct of rationalisation which attempts to show that industrial society itself rests on a peculiar notion of control. It is thus no accident that a positivist conception of social science which was tied to an engineering notion of theory and practice gained credence as industrial society developed, for it was just a conception which this society required for its continued existence. The idea of a positivist social science emerging into a policy science is to advance industrial society what liberal economic theory was to the early forms of *laissez-faire* capitalism. A positivist social science, technical control, and industrialism: these are mutually reinforcing features of modern social life.

38 For a richer account of these matters, one ought to read the brilliant essay by Jürgen Habermas, 'Technology and Science as Ideology', in *Towards a Rational Society*.

39 For a difficult but stimulating critique of Weber's account of the Western idea of reason and the development of industrial capitalism, and one which is supplementary to the thesis I am developing here, cf. H. Marcuse, 'Industrialisation and Capitalism in Max Weber', reprinted in *Negations*. There Marcuse examines the ways in which the process of rationalisation as Weber conceives it, and specifically its realisation in the capitalist mode of industrialisation, is necessarily tied up with certain forms of political and social domination. This is a theme I will take up in section 3.2.

Appendix

The most reasonable place to start in any historical review of the idea of a social science and its relation to political affairs is with the work of Henri Saint-Simon; unfortunately, only a small amount of the relevant material from his work is to be found in the only available English translation by

F. W. Markham, *Selected Writings*, and consequently I would recommend also reading the excellent intellectual biography of him by Frank Manuel, *The New World of Henri Saint-Simon*. This book will direct any interested reader to the predecessors of Saint-Simon, particularly Bacon (especially the *Novum Organum*, Part I and the *New Atlantis*), the Abbé Saint-Pierre (especially his *Observations on the Continuous Progress of the Universal Reason*), Turgot (especially the *Notes on a Universal History*), and Condorcet (particularly the *Sketch for a Historical Picture of the Progress of the Human Mind*). Auguste Comte gives the most complete statement of the positivist ideal in the nineteenth century; cf. particularly his 'The System of Positive Polity. A Plan of the Scientific Operations Necessary for Reorganising Society', as well as the more obvious *The Positive Philosophy*. John Stuart Mill's ideas on this subject are best found in Book VI, Chapter 12 of his major work, *System of Logic*, which is entitled, 'On the Logic of the Moral Sciences'. The positivist ideal is also interestingly developed by the American, Lester Ward (cf. his *Psychic Factors in Civilisation*).

The more modern period of what I call the positivist ideal really begins with the work of Durkheim and Weber. On Durkheim's ideas on the methodology of the social sciences, with some reference to its relevance to the reform of social life, cf. *The Rules of the Sociological Method* and the essays collected under the title, *Sociology and Philosophy*; however, to appreciate Durkheim's vision of modern society and the role which science has in it, one ought also to read *The Division of Labour in Society*, *Professional Ethics and Civic Morals*, and especially his commentary on Saint-Simon, *Socialism and Saint-Simon*. As far as Weber is concerned, besides the works I cite later on in Chapter 2, his basic ideas about the nature of social science and its uses can be found in the articles collected under the title *On Methodology of the Social Sciences* and his famous essay, 'Science as a Vocation' (in *From Max Weber*).

What might loosely be called the contemporary period is literally filled with books and articles which discuss the relation of social science to social practice in terms which resemble those I employ in Chapter 2 (and, in the light of what I say towards the end of this chapter about the relation of industrial society and social science positivistically conceived, this is no surprise). Here I will mention only a few which stand out for their lucidity or their fame: George Lundberg's *Can Science Save Us?*; Lady Barbara Wootton's *Testament for Social Science*; B. F. Skinner's *Beyond Freedom and Dignity* (also his novel, *Walden II*); Karl Mannheim, *Ideology and Utopia* (especially Part III, 'The Prospects of Scientific Politics'); Robert Lynd's *Knowledge for What*; Harold Lasswell's *Psychopathology and Politics* and *A Pre-view of Policy Sciences*; Karl Popper's *The Open Society and its Enemies*, Chapters 3 and 9, as well as *The Poverty of Historicism*; and George E. G. Catlin's *The Science and Method of Politics*.

There are a number of general commentaries on these matters which are well worth reading; among these are: F. A. Hayek, *The Counter-Revolution of Science*; L. Kolakowski, *The Alienation of Reason*; B. Crick, *The American Science of Politics*; R. Bendix, *Social Science and the Distrust of Reason*; the essays collected in H. Storing (ed.), *Essays on the Scientific Study of Politics*; and T. S. Simey, *Social Science and Social Purpose*.

3

Criticisms of the Positivist View of Social Science and Politics

3.1 *Ends and means*

The technological view of politics envisages the creation of a policy science, i.e. a set of scientific laws and axiomatic decision rules which a politician can use to determine objectively the best course of action to take. Of course, the policy scientist cannot make *all* of the necessary decisions scientifically, for, as I have already pointed out, any conception of the scientisation of politics must take account of the distinction between facts and values. This has been done by drawing another distinction between means and ends, the idea being the simple one that the choice of the ends to be pursued is thought to be a choice requiring a value judgement, but that the question as to the best means to a prescribed end is thought to be a factual question and therefore decidable scientifically. Thus it is that a policy scientist is thought to be competent only in deciding the 'best means', which is to say that the social policies he recommends are those which are instrumental to achieving certain posited ends.

Unfortunately, this neat identification of means questions and decisions with the factual side of the fact-value dichotomy is untenable, and because of this the whole notion of a policy scientist objectively choosing the best means to a prescribed end is an incoherent one. I will now demonstrate this, first, by introducing a qualification in order to show that a 'means-ends' analysis is more complicated than one might initially suppose, and, second, by developing a two-pronged argument which will

D

show that the idea of deciding the best means to a given end without invoking the particular values of the policy scientist rests on certain logical errors. If this indeed be the case, then a policy science as I have described it is in principle impossible.

The first point I want to make is really only a qualification of the simple scheme which identifies means questions as factual ones; it involves an analysis of the standards in terms of which the 'best' means are to be ascertained. For in order to choose a social policy a yardstick is required against which the various alternatives can be measured and compared, and on the basis of which one policy can be recommended over the others. Now those who advocate a policy science usually assume that it is the most efficient path which ought to be adopted, and consequently efficiency becomes the criterion in virtue of which the merits of various political measures will be assessed.[1] Unfortunately the concept of efficiency alone cannot provide an adequate standard in terms of which objective decisions can be made, for the concept of efficiency is a purely formal term signifying the ratio of amount of work performed to the total energy expended, and as such it can only have content, and therefore practical meaning, when one provides another standard in terms of which work and energy can be identified and measured.[2] Moreover, *this can only be done in terms of some already agreed upon value,* and this means that the concept of efficiency, when employed in the way envisioned by the policy scientist, is a value-laden concept. Thus, if a policy scientist were to advocate the adoption of the most efficient means to a given end, one would be forced to inquire, efficient in terms of what – monetary cost? human labour? suffering? the consumption of natural fuels? time? or what? For until this question is answered there is literally no way

[1] My arguments could quite easily be extended to cover the host of similar concepts used to give meaning to the word 'best' in the phrase 'best means': concepts such as 'economical', 'workable', 'profitable', 'functional', 'convenient', etc.

[2] There is another way of formulating the concept of efficiency, and this is 'maximising overall goal attainment' such that the most efficient means is the one which is most compatible with the preference orderings of the politician who sets the end of the policy. Regardless of the fact that this would require a complete specification of his preferences over all relevant possible states of the world, even if this could be done my point here would still stand, namely, that *the standard in terms of which the 'best means' is to be defined necessarily incorporates certain particular values.*

of choosing between alternative courses in terms of efficiency. And the point here is that *whatever* answer one gives will reflect a judgement as to that set of factors which the policy scientist thinks is the most important in situations of this type, a judgement that cannot be scientifically made for it involves reference to the *values* of the scientist.

So it is that a policy science that attempts to provide a structure in terms of which political questions could be settled 'rationally' must involve reference to just those considerations that the idea of policy science was designed to eliminate, namely, notions of significance and worth. As a result, debates between policy scientists about the most efficient means would still be inherently 'political' in the sense that the choice of standards of what is to count as evidence and proof of some social policy being the 'best' (in this case, the meaning of the criterion of efficiency) would necessarily reflect the values of the disputants.

But this is still only a *qualification* of the idea of a policy science, not an argument to show that such an idea is incoherent, because it is possible for one to admit that the standards which the policy scientist employs must be given to him by the politician who makes decisions about values, and still also claim that, given these standards, the policy scientist can objectively decide the best means to a given end. In other words, all my argument demonstrates is that the 'value-framework' within which the policy scientist operates is more extensive than at first supposed – for it now includes standards of judgement as well as goals. Within the admittedly more constricted region defined by this framework, however, the policy scientist can practice his trade.

Actually, although the above argument really only introduces a qualification of the notion of a policy science, it does lead into a much stronger argument, one which *does* demonstrate that the idea of a value-neutral policy science is an incoherent one. This argument is related to the difficulty of drawing a sharp and enduring distinction between what is an end and what is a means. For every means is an end relative to the means required to achieve it, so that any given course of action may be either a means or an end depending upon the point of view which one adopts. Now I said that the argument against the idea of scientifically selecting the best means is *related* to the relativity of ends and means, and it is so in this way: all policy scientists are willing to admit that the ends of action reflect the values of the person who chooses this end, but they maintain that the means to this end are all value-neutral, and that their worth is to be decided solely in terms of their instrumental value, of their contribution to the achievement of a given end; but if any particular course of action can be either a means or an end, then it must be the case that even a so-called 'means' reflects the values and life-commitments of the person who supports it, since this means is itself an end from another perspective. Thus, questions of means to ends, as much as questions about the ends themselves, are decidable only by reference to the values of the questioners.

And, upon reflection, this seems an obvious point. For all political decisions, even those which are seen as means to an end, are social policies, and as such they embody a notion of what people ought to be required or permitted to do to others. No social policy's worth can be solely instrumental because any such policy will require that people interact with one another in certain definite ways, and for this reason it must have a moral value *in itself*. This can be shown most effectively by the sorts of criticisms that are open to one regarding so-called technical proposals for the best means. What if it were concluded that the most efficient (i.e. the cheapest, fastest, most simple, etc.) way to deal with the population problem were simply to exterminate large numbers of some special class of people?[3] The point is that such a proposal could be objected to not simply on the grounds of technical efficiency, but also on the basis of an antipathy to the moral values inherent in it. *All* political proposals, no matter how instrumental, will alter and shape the personal relations of at least some of the members of a society, and will affect the relative welfare of various classes of people; as such they embody moral notions as to what is permissable, just, or right in human affairs. They are a species of moral statement.

Nor will it do to try and make the same sort of move which was made above by introducing the idea of 'normative con-

[3] Cf. J. Swift's *A Modest Proposal for Preventing the Poor People in Ireland from Being a Burden to Their Parents and for Making them Beneficial to the Public.* Swift is, of course, making the same point I am through very heavy irony. There are some Catholics who argue that legalised abortion to solve the population problem is in the same category.

straints' which delimit the area within which the policy scientist is able to function (such constraints being given to him, along with the goals and standards I discussed above, by the politician). For the point is that even within such a framework the decisions of the policy scientist would be shot through and through with his values, and this can be seen in terms of the argument I have just made. The policies the scientist recommends will still reflect his views about how people ought to live together, and they therefore can be disputed on moral as well as technical grounds. Thus, perhaps the elimination of classes of people would be prohibited because of the 'normative constraints' given to the policy scientist by the politician, and the scientist might therefore propose mass sterilisation instead; but this could be rejected because of the value of free choice, for example, and then he would be forced to recommend another policy, say a programme of economic incentives to influence people in various ways; but this might also be questioned because it seems to be inegalitarian, affecting the poorer classes more than the rich; and so he might propose a policy of ... etc., etc. No matter what social policy he offers as the best means to achieving the end of stabilising the population (which is itself probably a means to achieving other ends, e.g. a minimum standard of income for all the citizens), it can be questioned on moral grounds precisely because all social policies incorporate a moral standpoint. Attempts at bracketing values away from social policies by making them part of the framework within which the policy scientist must operate would result, in the last analysis, in making it impossible for the policy scientist to propose anything!

In fact this argument can be taken even one step further. Assume what I have in fact tried to deny, namely, that a policy scientist could impartially determine the most efficient means to a given end; still my argument runs, to engage in this type of political decision-making itself betrays a certain conception of the purposes and needs of men which the political sphere is supposed to satisfy, and it therefore incorporates certain values. In fact, just because proposals regarding a certain instrumental course of action based on a policy scientific analysis presuppose a theory of politics which incorporates certain values, such proposals themselves cannot be politically neutral.

Perhaps the best way of demonstrating this is to characterise another theory of politics which is inimical to the technological view which I have described, and whose realisation would be foreclosed if a policy science were established. This alternative theory might be termed the Aristotelean conception of politics.[4] Briefly, according to this view what is important in political decision-making is not only the end result that is produced – a certain allocation of men and resources or a new rule, for example – but the process by which such authoritative decisions are made. More specifically, according to this theory 'politics' refers to men's deliberate efforts to order, direct, and control their collective affairs and activities, to establish ends for their society, and to implement and evaluate these ends. From this perspective, what is fundamental about politics is the interaction and participation of men according to mutually defined and accepted rules as they engage in this process of creating and administering the laws of their community, which is to say that what is most significant is the involvement of the citizens in the process of determining their own collective identity. For, it is argued, men are self-conscious creatures who can reflect on their experiences and actions and on the arrangements by which they order their lives, and who can, on the basis of this self-reflection, change the way they live; human consciousness thus implies a process of self-formation in which new forms of experience and action are made possible because one has reflected on his past experience and action. Political activity must be understood as this very same process undertaken by the members of the group with respect to their group identity; in other words, politics is to collective affairs what the striving for autonomy is to personal matters. And it is for this reason that men can be free only when they participate in determining the conditions of their lives, and are not simply subject to the commands of others: for to be deprived of the opportunities for political participation is to lose the chance to exercise one's powers of self-reflection, and, as a result, to lose the essential human capacity of self-determination with regard to some of the most important areas of our existence; and one can be free only when one is self-determining.

Moreover, this tradition also emphasises the social character

[4] Such a conception is not limited to Aristotle, of course; it can be found in Rousseau, Hegel, and Marx as well. For a contemporary account, cf. H. Arendt, *The Human Condition*.

of men's self-consciousness, claiming that the ideas men have of themselves, of what is appropriate, right, and fitting, of what their abilities and capacities are, of what they are worth and what they ought to value and aspire towards – all of these ideas which comprise men's images of themselves are a function of the social world in which they live. For men become self-conscious in the process of becoming members of a social order, learning its language, adopting its standards of excellence and importance, and comparing themselves to the other men in their society. What each person is results in large part from what other men think him to be. It is because of this aspect of human consciousness that political argument, persuasion, and action are thought to be fundamental aspects of human life, for it is in these sorts of activities that men self-consciously reveal themselves to others and in the process learn who they are and what they want. Political life is thus an indispensable element in the process of becoming and being a person.

Now there are a number of institutional features which must characterise any political arrangement designed to foster this kind of activity, and most of these have to do with making possible free and uncoerced communication among the citizens. It is not possible to discuss these here; but there is one such feature which cannot be present, and this is that political decisions should be made by a group of technically trained experts. For such a situation would obviously make impossible the sort of political activity I have been describing – it would be a form of autocracy in which decisions were imposed on the members. In this regard it is worthwhile to remember Aristotle's remark that one of the ways that the polis can be destroyed is through the excessive unity which stems from having 'correct' solutions imposed on it by either philosophers or kings.

The point of all this regarding the notion of a policy science with which one is supposed to be able to ascertain impartially the best means to a given end can be made very simply: by deciding to turn one's political problems over to a policy scientist, one thereby closes off a type of political life which is rooted in a different conception of human needs and purposes, so that to accept the idea of a policy science is to accept a certain set of values and to reject others. The policy scientist does not act in a neutral and impartial manner, eschewing all value-judgements, for his very activity incorporates certain values which his proposals necessarily presuppose and reflect.

These are a few of the ways in which conceiving of instrumental questions as if they were entirely factual, and consequently thinking that proposals as to the best means are based on purely technical considerations, is fundamentally misleading. Questions as to the best means necessarily involve and express certain basic values on the part of the policy scientist, and it is for this reason that the demand for such a science is in principle unrealisable. There is no way to eliminate the distinctly political element from political questions, and the attempt to do so itself only ironically reveals certain deep political evaluations. In the next section, in fact, I will attempt to elucidate the substantive character of these values.

Before this, however, I want to remark on an often heard complaint to the effect that those who reject the possibility of a policy science want to have their cake and eat it too, because they argue both that a policy science is impossible and that it is dangerous; surely, the complaint runs, a policy science can only be dangerous if it exists, and if it can not exist then why worry about it? But this complaint fails to distinguish between an activity and the characterisation of this activity. Just because the notion of a policy science is logically incoherent, it does not follow that one has nothing to fear from the *idea* of such a science; for even though such a science is in theory impossible, the idea of it may still retain its power, and men who make essentially political decisions of an instrumentalist sort may still call themselves policy scientists because they think that they are indeed offering neutral, merely technical, advice. Political advisers can mischaracterise their activities and these mischaracterisations can continue to have enormous power and influence; in this case, the mischaracterisations involved in claiming that political decisions are really 'only technical' may serve to hide the fundamentally evaluative elements in these decisions, thereby helping to promote the establishment and/or continuance of these evaluative elements by removing them, in effect, from public discussion. By showing that a policy science is a logical impossibility one has not thereby eliminated the dangers inherent in the idea of a policy science.[5] However, what these specific dangers are can only be appreciated by examining the basic ideology which the idea of a policy science incorporates, and it is to this that I now turn.

3.2 *Ideological content: support for industrial society*[6]

A policy science is supposed to be a device for organising political thought in a rational way, merely a method for clarifying empirical relationships among alternative actions and for sorting out their likely consequences, and a procedure for making 'correct' decisions; as such, it is supposed to be employable by anyone, regardless of his political views, for any end whatsoever, and its results are supposed to be impartial in the sense of not being dependent upon the particular evaluations of the policy scientist for their truth. Now in the preceding section I argued that any recommendation that a policy scientist might make would necessarily incorporate within it certain, perhaps implicit, political evaluations, which is to say that such a scientist cannot make impartial political decisions. In this section I want to extend this formal point by examining some of the actual values that are inherent in the whole policy scientific approach. The self-consciously positivist ideal that I have described actually structures political analysis in certain definite ways, and it

[5] There is another danger which, because I am not discussing the epistemological claims of the positivist model of social science here, I will simply mention. It is that it might be the case that social science cannot provide genuinely nomological laws, and therefore the policy scientific planning of the type the positivist model envisions is doomed to failure. The danger here is that, in so far as a society comes to depend for the solution of its problems on the existence of a policy science, these problems would go unsolved. The disparity between an industrial society's requirement for planning and the ability of social science to provide the means by which such planning is to be implemented would pose a great threat to such a society's continued existence if this disparity could not be overcome.

[6] For supplementary reading to this section, one ought to consult Georg Lukács, *Class and Class Consciousness*, especially the essay 'Reification and the Consciousness of the Proletariat'; Max Horkheimer, *The Eclipse of Reason*; Max Horkheimer and Theodor Adorno, *Dialectic of Enlightenment*; Herbert Marcuse, *One Dimensional Man*; and Jürgen Habermas, *Theory and Practice*, especially the last essay, 'On Theory and Praxis in our Civilisation', and *Towards a Rational Society*, especially the essay, 'Technology and Science as Ideology'.

thereby fosters an attitude towards social problems which is expressed in the sort of conclusions that a so-called policy scientist might propose. It is in this way that a viewpoint that claims to be a non-political method, indifferent to the specific political views of those who employ it, becomes an ideology when it enters the political realm.

I will now examine this ideological content by demonstrating how the policy scientific approach is biased towards supporting the basic features of industrial society. In order to do this I will have to consider four specific aspects of the idea of a policy science, but it will only be at the end of the discussion, when it will be possible to show how these aspects are interrelated, that the ideological content of the positivist programme can be fully appreciated.

The first point which is necessary to make is a historical one, and this is that the idea of a policy science arose, and has been embedded, only in the context of industrial society. In section 2.2 I gave reasons why this should have been the case, when I discussed the process of rationalisation as a characteristic feature of modern industrial society. There I made the point that an industrial form of social organisation is rooted in the same sorts of ideas as those which give rise to the notion of a policy science – nowhere is this more clearly expressed than in the writings of Saint-Simon which I mentioned in the Appendix to Chapter 2 – and that this form of organisation also reinforces the policy scientific ideal by its viewing people and their social relations in terms of their instrumental value, and its requiring technical control over social processes. It is in the context of an industrial society that one finds the idea that there must be the conscious manipulation of social relationships according to some set of laws and established procedures in order to maximise political and economic efficiency.

Now this is an important fact when considering the second aspect regarding the idea of a policy science, namely, that the positivist social science upon which it is based necessarily reifies the basic social institutions and customs of the society it is studying. 'Reification' means 'making into a thing', and it refers to the tendency of taking what are essentially conventional activities and treating them as if they were natural entities which have a separate existence of their own, and which operate according to a given set of laws independently of the wishes of the social actors who engage in them.

Why is it the case that a policy science implies a reification of the basic features of the society in which it is operating? It does so because a policy science requires a set of general laws of society in accordance with which situations will be manipulated in order to produce a given end. This means that it assumes that the social world, like the natural world, is comprised of a set of primitive, regular relationships which men must operate in terms of in order to avoid catastrophe. In other words, the laws of social life are assumed by a policy science to have a separate power which can only be dealt with by ascertaining what these laws are and regulating one's actions accordingly. This assumption is expressed clearly in Comte's notion of 'wise resignation', as well as in Popper's discussion of piecemeal social engineering, both of which I mentioned in section 2.1.

This means that a policy science, in requiring a set of general laws of society, views social relations as if they were processes which have a life of their own and which function in the way they do regardless of the wishes of the actors who engage in them – processes which have a power over and against these social actors. This is exactly what Marx, in discussing the phenomenon of alienation, called reification,[7] that is, the giving to what are essentially the creations of one's own activity a separate, alien existence which have sway over one and to which one must give obedience, as in the ideas of God, the state, and 'fetishised commodities'. From this perspective it ought to be clear that the policy scientific approach gives to the social order – which is nothing more than the conventional activities of its members, together with their beliefs, expectations, and desires – the qualities of an object which exists irrespective of the ideas of men. Here what is reified is either the basic structures of the society being studied, those fundamental institutions, customs, habits, and ideas which give to this society its distinctive identity (in the case of laws which are applicable to a given society), or certain recurring structural relationships (in the case of laws which pur-

[7] Cf. the analysis of alienation in terms of the concept of reification in Georg Lukács, *Class and Class Consciousness*. Thus, in so far as what I say is true, one could claim that the belief in the idea of a policy science is a form of alienation.

portedly apply to all forms of social organisation, and which are instantiated in the society under question in some way). In both instances, a policy science necessarily must treat some aspects of a particular social situation as simply given, beyond political evaluation and control, just because it is only in terms of these 'basic aspects' that he is able to make his calculations.

Thus it is that a policy science must accept certain basic social arrangements as *necessarily*[8] the way they are, and, by making his proposals in terms of their continued existence, he thereby unwittingly acts to support these very arrangements. And it is for this reason that, in the context of industrial society, a policy science, by operating in terms of its basic arrangements and proposing policies in accordance with them, contains an ideological bias in support of this particular form of social organisation.

An example of such reification would be this one taken from economic policy-making. Keynesian economics says, in effect, 'this is the way that the economy functions – these are the "laws of the economic system", with interest rates, liquidity preferences, the consumption function, levels of aggregate investment, etc., etc., interrelating according to the following scheme. Now, assuming that one wishes to raise the level of employment, this is the best way to proceed. . . .' The point here is that the so-called 'laws of the economic system' are taken to be natural necessities like gravity, with the effect that the relationships which these laws describe are taken as given parameters within which the specified problem of employment must be solved. But this has the unwitting effect of reinforcing certain structural features of a particular form of industrial capitalism.

The major result of this process of reification is that it limits the horizons of possible political action by circumscribing the area within which one can act politically. This same circumspec-

[8] Of course, all reasoned attempts to formulate a policy must treat some aspects of a situation as given; what distinguishes the policy scientific approach is that, because it views society as governed by natural laws, it must view certain aspects of the situation as unalterable. In other words, in the policy scientific approach there are certain basic elements of the social structure which are 'mere givens' and which serve as the unquestionable parameters of policy making.

tion is also the upshot of a third feature of the idea of a policy science, and this is the impoverishment of political discussion that would occur if a policy scientific approach came to permeate the political order.

The idea of a policy science rests on the twin assumptions that only a scientific approach in political life can ensure a rational solution to political problems, and that only questions of means, or instrumental questions, are amenable to a scientific solution. Combining these two assumptions forces one to conclude that problems about the ends of political life are matters undebatable in a rational manner and therefore not worthy of consideration. The idea of a policy science rests on the conviction that debates about political principles and ideals, imaginative efforts to picture alternative worlds, arguments about the basic values which particular social institutions ought to incorporate and foster, that all of these are mere 'metaphysical speculation', 'expressions of preference', 'self-assertive decisions', and so on. Questions not accessible to a so-called technical analysis are thought to be irrational, and therefore essentially undiscussable.

In this atmosphere, political inquiry and discussion would be levelled out, restricted to technical questions of finding out the most efficient means of achieving a goal of policy. Analyses antagonistic both to the style and substance of the policy scientific approach would be ignored, omitted from serious consideration; and questions as to the worth or value of a particular social order would be denied validity. The conservative effect of this ought to be clear. The options of the actors in a given society would be drastically limited because critiques of the ends or assumptions or values of that society could not be seriously engaged in – such questions would be conceived as being 'merely subjective'. It is for this reason that, arising within the framework of an industrial society, a policy scientific approach to political life would tend to reinforce the continued existence of such a society.

The fourth aspect of the idea of a policy science which is germane to a discussion of its ideological content is that, in a society which is characterised by dominant-submissive social relations (in the sense that there are those people or classes of people who characteristically make decisions of basic social significance and those for whom decisions are made – and this is the case in an industrial society), such a science would almost inevitably be supportive of those who are dominant. The reason for this is that the operation of a policy science presupposes that those employing this approach, or their agents, have the power to manipulate variables to produce the results in the way the policy science calls for, and it is thus only useful to those who have control over the relevant variables. Now it will usually be the case, though not necessarily so, that those who are in power are also those who have the power to control the relevant variables.

The inherent tendency to support the dominant elements in a social order is reinforced when one places the idea of a policy science within the concrete social setting of modern industrial society. For in a society which is dedicated to an efficient functioning of the processes of production, and to which technology is useful only in so far as it enables this process to continue in an orderly and progressive fashion, then a social technology would come to be thought as primarily useful in maintaining this system. But in so far as this system is rooted in dominant-submissive social relations, this technology would thus only go to strengthen and reinforce this type of social relationship.

The basic conservatism *vis-à-vis* industrial society of the idea of a policy science can be seen in the ways in which the four features I have been discussing interact with one another to support the *status quo* of an industrial society. For example, it is interesting to see how the tendencies towards reification and towards buttressing the hold of dominant groups join together to foster a repression of certain kinds of political discussion, which in turn reinforces the domination of certain groups, thereby producing a vicious circle. In so far as the idea of a policy science gained credence in an industrial society, basic social relations would thus be taken to be 'objectively required' (because of reification), and thus given an independent status; this would mean, among other things, that the members of the society who are dominated could not see that their society was rooted in a domination which was not necessary but only conventional. Their language and their understanding of themselves and their society would consist of concepts which reflected this illusion, but they would know nothing about this because they would have neither the vocabulary nor the perspective to discuss their true relationships; they would think that their relationships, which are obviously and openly inegalitarian, had to be the way they were, that they were natural and 'given'. The dominated could not see the dominance of those in control as coercive or thwarting because they would have become prisoners of a set of ideas which leads seemingly rational, if implicit, support to these inegalitarian social institutions.

Moreover, what is more important is that until the actors came to see their social order as repressive there is no reason to expect that its dominant-submissive structure would disappear, except by accident. The reason for this is that social relations are relations which are defined and regulated in terms of duties, rights, obligations, rewards, responsibilities, roles, and so on, i.e. they are fundamentally conceptual relations which form part of a cultural tradition of communication; thus, until the social actors came to speak of themselves and their society differently, i.e. to employ different concepts in their relations with others, no sort of liberation from a society rooted in domination could occur. *But it is the repression of just this sort of discussion which the ideology of a policy science fosters,* and it thereby helps to maintain the illusions without which a society based on domination could not continue.

How this might work out in actual practice can be seen by amplifying the example taken from economics which I introduced above. In so far as the belief of economists that they are discovering the 'laws of the economic system' was accepted as true in a society, the members of this society – including those who were in the 'lower orders', i.e. those who did not make socially important economic decisions – would think of the basic structures of production and distribution of goods and services typical of their society as necessary and given, as part of the nature of industrialism. There would be the widespread belief that there was a natural order of social life with which people had to get in line, and that this order was discovered by social scientists; and such a belief would contribute to the members of this social order accepting the inequality of power which was an enduring feature of their lives, for they would view it as something over which they had no choice. They would not see the dominance of certain people *as coercive,* any more than they would see the natural fact that they need air as coercive; both would be givens of existence.

Furthermore, in so far as the science of economics was accompanied by a call for a policy science – the idea being that only scientific reasoning is rational – and in so far as this call was limited to those instrumental questions of the best means to a given end, than the very notion that there are rationally possible alternatives to the form of industrial life which they were living, would be precluded even before the discussion ever got started. The reason for this is simple: the convergence of both these factors discredits a fundamental questioning of the basic arrangements of society as irrational. The upshot of this is that those who are in a dominated position cannot come to see that they need not be in this position, that there are viable alternatives to their situation, that they can change their lot in an intelligent, coherent manner. Without knowing it, they are forced to accept a situation which they need not accept; they are trapped, not only by their social order, but also by their own ideas.

Reification, the impoverishment of political discussion, and political domination are latent features in the idea of a policy science which interlock and reinforce one another, thereby forming a strong force which, in contemporary terms, helps to maintain the structure of industrial society. Far from being politically neutral, as its proponents claim, the idea of a policy science is one of the deep, important, and enduring ideologies of our own time, one which is all the stronger in that it claims to be 'objective' and 'scientific'. Unmasking the ideological content of this doctrine is therefore not just an exercise in philosophical analysis, but a move to open up the possibility for a social order along quite different lines from our own.

3.3 *Its philosophy of social science*

Even though I have argued that a positivist conception of social science is conceptually tied to an engineering, policy scientific view of theory and practice, the criticisms of section 3.2, while they may be telling from a certain political point of view, do not appear to offer compelling reasons for abandoning the positivist model of social science. For this would be like arguing that evolution is wrong because it leads to a decline in trust of the Bible, or that science is in error because it tends to subvert political authority based on magical practices. All that the argument has so far shown is that, in so far as there is a conceptual link between a positivist account of social science and the idea of a policy science, there is an inherent ideological element in the positivist model of social science; and this does not demonstrate that the model itself is fallacious.

Or does it? For one should remember that the positivist position is one that claims that it is non-ideological, i.e. it claims to be different from all other approaches to understanding human behaviour, social institutions and history in that it is value-free, that its truths neither presuppose nor entail certain judgements on the part of the social scientist in order for his statements to be true. Earlier I characterised this claim as the belief in the ethical neutrality of the social sciences, and I tried to show that this was a central pillar of the positivist model, one that underlay the very possibility of a social science as conceived by the proponents of this model. But now it appears that the positivist model *does* rest on a certain conception of politics, man and society, and that, indeed, it is in terms of this conception that what is to count as evidence, truth, a descriptive term, and so on, is determined by this conception. Possible instrumental control constitutes the grounds for the claims to validity of such a science, and the rationalisation of certain social practices is one of its effects.

But this means that the positivist's understanding of the role that values play in social science is inaccurate, which means, in turn, that his conception of social science cannot be correct. It is in this way that one can argue from the political consequences of the positivist model to the position that the positivist model is itself at fault, that its account of the nature of social science is wrong.

Now this is not to claim that I have hereby *shown* in what ways the positivist account is in error – I have only shown how one might *begin* to argue that such an account is fallacious. In order to make this claim genuine it would be necessary to construct a full account of precisely how the values of the scientist are expressed in his descriptions and explanations, and how the acceptance or rejection of his accounts is in part a function of one's acceptance or rejection of these values. This is clearly a task far beyond this book; but at least it indicates one way in which one might proceed from an examination of the relationship between theory and practice into an examination of the theory of knowledge which inevitably supports any particular view of this relationship.

Actually, in recent times there has been a great deal of thought devoted to questions regarding the foundations of social science and its relationship to other forms of knowledge, and especially to a re-examination of the positivist model which I have been considering. The first source of this thought has been in analytic philosophy in the last fifteen years.[9] Philosophers here have sought to drive a wedge between the understanding of people and the understanding of things by engaging in a conceptual analysis of the various types of concepts which are employed in the social sciences, attempting to ascertain what one is logically committed to as a result of using these concepts.[10] In particular, the debate has centred on the logic of action concepts and the role of interpretation in descriptions;[11] the role of *verstehen* explanations even in quasi-causal[12] and functional[13] explanations; the nature of causal explanation in social science,[14] and whether explanations in terms of intentions, motives, and desires are of this variety;[15] and finally the role that models of man play in the basic theoretical frameworks of social science.[16]

These analyses are still in an incomplete state;[17] nevertheless, there does seem to be a genuinely new impetus afoot to integrate them with the findings of two related sources. The first of these is the new accounts of the nature of science that are being given in the philosophy of science as a result of new interpretations of the nature of meaning[18] and the role of conceptual frameworks in

[9] I say fifteen years because it was in 1957–8 that Peter Winch's *Idea of a Social Science* and William Dray's *Laws and Explanation in History* were published. Needless to say, these are still the texts which set the terms of the argument in the philosophy of social science.

[10] Cf. C. Taylor, *The Explanation of Behaviour*, and A. R. Louch, *Explanation and Human Action.*

[11] C. Taylor, 'Interpretation and the Sciences of Man', *Review of Metaphysics*, Sept. 1971.

[12] Cf. G. H. Von Wright, *Explanation and Understanding*, esp. ch. 4.

[13] Cf. D. Emmett, *Functions, Purposes, and Powers.*

[14] Cf. A. MacIntyre, 'The Idea of a Social Science'.

[15] Cf. A. MacIntyre, 'A Mistake about Causality in Social Science'.

[16] Cf. P. Winch, 'Understanding a Primitive Society'.

[17] Cf. The volume edited by R. Borger and F. Cioffi, *Explanation and the Behavioural Sciences.*

[18] Cf. P. K. Feyerabend, 'Explanation, Reduction, and Empiricism', in *Minnesota Studies*, vol. 3.

scientific inquiry.[19] Of particular importance is the examination of the nature of a theory and how it relates to laws, models, analogies, and conceptual frameworks,[20] and to the age-old discussion about the neutrality and objectivity of observation statements.[21] As an example of how this has affected the philosophy of social science, there is the new discussion of the role paradigms play in social science.[22]

The second source has been the recent entrance into the debate – from the viewpoint of the English-speaking world, of course – of the critical Marxism of the Frankfurt school.[23] Actually, the relevance of this work to that being carried on within analytic philosophy has only become apparent recently. The reason for this is that the debates within analytic philosophy have led up to a point at which the work in phenomenology and hermeneutics has become pertinent,[24] and it is with this tradition that the Frankfurt school has carried on its debates. It is as if it now remains the task of the analytic philosophy of social science to internalise and express in its own terms the sorts of arguments that have been considered in other contexts.[25] This of course does not mean that it will merely recapitulate these other philosophies, for, in the first place, it has entirely different roots,[26] and, in the second place, it will presumably be critical of many of

19 Cf. T. Kuhn, *The Structure of Scientific Revolutions.*

20 Cf. S. Korner, *Categorial Frameworks*, and *Experience and Theory*; I. Lakatos, 'Falsification and the Methodology of Scientific Research Programmes' in Lakatos and Musgrave, *Criticism and the Growth of Knowledge*, pp. 91–195.

21 Cf. I. Scheffler, *Science and Subjectivity.*

22 Cf. S. Wolin, 'Paradigms and Political Theories', in *Politics and Experience.*

23 Cf. J. Habermas, *Knowledge and Human Interests*, *Theory and Practice*, and *Towards a Rational Society*; K. O. Apel, *Analytic Philosophy and the Geisteswissenschaften*; A. Wellmer, *Critical Theory of Society*; K. O. Apel, 'The *A Priori* of Communication and the Foundation of the Humanities', *Man and World*, vol. 5, no. 1.

24 Cf., e.g. C. Taylor, 'Interpretation and the Sciences of Man'.

25 This is one way of considering the criticisms that Gellner makes of Winch regarding the analysis of irrational social practices in his 'Concepts and Society'. Cf. the entire volume in which this is reprinted, B. Wilson (ed.), *Rationality*. Much of what I write in section 4.3 and Chapter 5 has been directly influenced by the work of Apel and Habermas.

26 In the philosophy of meaning rather than the philosophy of consciousness, for example.

their claims in the process of trying to come to terms with them.

It really does seem that a genuine synthesis is in the making[27] in which the foundations of the social sciences will be reset in a mould radically different from the positivist model that I have been analysing. Only the most unreflective social scientist would fail to realise that the very basis of the positivist account of the social sciences has been severely shaken,[28] and, with it, the engineering view of social theory's relationship to political practice.

While these analyses I have just described have approached the question of the scientific standing of social science from the standpoint of the philosophy of social science, I have been concerned to approach this matter from another direction, namely, from the viewpoint of political philosophy. It is possible for these separate approaches to converge on the same point precisely because there is a logical connection between a view as to the nature of social theory and a view as to how social theory is related to political practice. Questions about the foundations of our knowledge of human behaviour naturally lead forward to questions about the use of this knowledge, and vice versa. The conventional practice of viewing knowledge on the one hand, and the use of this knowledge on the other, as conceptually distinct is fundamentally misguided.

It is on the basis of these considerations that another point immediately follows; it is that it is overwhelmingly important *to see the political, i.e. socially relevant, dimension of the arguments about the nature of social science*. This point has obviously been recognised by all those in the Marxist tradition, but it is *not* one that is generally recognised in the traditions of either mainstream social science – where the debates are thought to concern only methodological questions – or of analytic philosophy – which still seeks to view philosophy as merely 'clearing up conceptual muddles' with no particular relevance to social life. These views are really quite inaccurate. For what is at stake

[27] Cf. R. Bernstein, *Praxis and Action*; G. Radnitzsky, *Contemporary Schools of Metascience*.

[28] Though it is true that the upshot of all this energy and discussion is still not completely clear. For the single best overview of all these matters in the philosophy of social science, cf. the long article by J. D. Moon, 'The Logic of Political Inquiry', in F. Greenstein and N. Polsby (eds), *Handbook of Political Science*.

in the debate as to the nature of social science is a view of man and society which has profound political repercussions, and nowhere is this clearer than in the views concerning the relation of theory to practice which are part and parcel of this debate, if only implicitly. What this book does in drawing together models of social science and notions of theory's relation to practice is to show how the philosophy of social science really gains its deepest human meaning when set inside the broader framework of political philosophy.

These points can be seen even more clearly when the existence of alternative models of social science and their associated conceptions of the relationship of theory to practice is recognised. At this point, therefore, I will present two alternative models of social science which have correspondingly different notions of how theory and practice are related. Perhaps then, by providing a contrast, the particular political and philosophical assumptions of positivism in social science will become more apparent. But, even more important, perhaps in so doing an outline of a way out of its difficulties will also have become clear.

4

An Alternative View: Interpretive Social Science

In this chapter I want to examine an alternative to the positivist theory which I have so far been considering. I will be able to provide only a brief description of it, partially because my purpose here is simply to offer a contrast, but also because the philosophical exploration of this alternative is at an incomplete state at the present time.

Speaking of a philosophical exploration leads me to an important caveat regarding the account I shall give in this chapter and in the next, when I discuss the idea of a critical social science. It is that while I will be employing the names 'interpretive social science' and 'critical social science' I will not be simply reproducing the accounts that are given by many of the theorists who self-consciously identify themselves by means of these names. I will not, for example, be trying to elucidate Schutz's *The Phenomenology of the Social World* when I discuss 'interpretive theory', or regurgitating Habermas's ideas when I examine 'critical theory'; indeed, in some respects I will be offering accounts which differ from theirs in important ways. My reasons for this are two-fold: in the first place I want to ground my accounts in a philosophical theory of meaning rather than in some other philosophical base (and thus my accounts develop out of the tradition of analytic philosophy rather than those of phenomenology or Marxist dialectics); and, in the second place, I think that what has been written in these other traditions is obscure or wrong-headed in some significant areas, and that it is because of this, among other reasons, that these other approaches have so often been dismissed. I hope that by proceeding in this manner my accounts will be lucid and plausible. Of course, and I want to emphasise this, such accounts are no substitute for the real and difficult work of systematically and vigorously pursuing a philosophical analysis of what it means to understand social behaviour; what I offer here are simply brief sketches.

In this chapter I will: first, give an exposition of the nature of interpretive social science; second, explicate the notion of theory and practice which is implied by, and which supports, this view of social science; and third, offer some fundamental criticisms of this approach.

4.1 *The idea of an interpretive social science*

The interpretive approach to social science, as constructed from the viewpoint of analytic philosophy, starts with the fact that a large part of the vocabulary of social science is comprised of *action concepts,* and it attempts to give an account of social science by examining the logical implications of employing this class of concepts. Action concepts are all those terms that are used to describe doings as opposed to happenings, so that 'jumping' is an action concept while 'falling' is not – jumping is something that someone does, whereas falling is something that happens to one. A way of understanding what an action concept is is to think of the difference between a leaf waving in the breeze and a person waving his hand. Action concepts are employed to describe behaviour which is done with a purpose such that one can ask, what is its point, aim or intent, or what was the person trying to do, desiring or meaning. Examples of action concepts are: buying, bribing, promising, hiking, voting, handshaking, and speaking. It is these concepts which go to make up the data which the social scientist seeks to explain.

There is an immediately obvious and yet extremely important point regarding the use of action concepts, and this is that the criteria for the application of these terms involve more than the mere observation of physical movements; in fact, they require an *interpretation* on the part of the observer. The reason for this is that any action concept involves reference to either the subject's intentions, plans or, desires (these are called 'intentional action concepts', and an example of one is the concept 'waiting'), or such things as the moral, legal, or social rules in accordance with which the subject is acting (these are called 'conventional action concepts', and an example of one is the concept 'voting'), and neither of these two features can be identified simply by reference to physical movements. For no physical movement is ever a necessary condition for an action – think of the myriads of ways in which one can vote, for example – simply because the aims which an action is intended to achieve can always be accomplished in literally countless ways; moreover, no physical movement can ever be a sufficient condition for a specific action to be said to have occurred because it is only in certain circumstances that particular movements can count as an action of a certain sort – thus, for example, saying 'I do' in front of a priest and one's fiancé, may be an act of marriage and it may not, depending on the circumstances, for the participants may be pretending or acting in a movie or rehearsing the ceremony, and so on. What specific action is being undertaken depends upon the meanings that the bodily movements being performed have.

This point about the relationship between interpretation and the description of an action immediately raises the question as to how descriptions of actions are related to their explanation. For if any action is a physical movement performed for a purpose such that its description involves implicit reference to the *point* of the action, then it seems that such a description also contains an explanatory element within it. In describing actions we are also making clear the intentions of the actor, which is to say that we are revealing the meaning that the act had for the actor. However, this does not mean that by giving a single description of an act one has thereby explained it, such that one cannot ask, why did he *do* X?; any action may have many descriptions which place it in a wider and wider context of purposes, intentions, and rules, so that one can ask, why did he do X?, and get an answer which consists of a 'higher-level' description. A man may be opening the window, but at the same time and with the same movements he may also be cooling the room, signalling to an accomplice outside, demonstrating a new sort of window, showing off his strength, and so on. Any action will have many consequences, some of which the agent may be intending to bring about, and it is for this reason that one can always seek to discover the *further intention* which the agent possessed beyond the one contained in the initial action description, and these further intentions will be expressed in the redescription of the act that one gives. It is these redescriptions which constitute explanations of the act described at a lower intentional level: 'why did he shoot the gun?' – to kill that man; 'why did he kill that man?' – to protect the president from an assassination.

One of the major tasks of an interpretive social science is to discover the intentions which actors have in doing whatever it is they are doing. This has historically been called a *verstehen* explanation, and this term would be fine except for the gross confusions that surround it. The term arose in the context of a rigid dualism in the philosophy of mind, in which intentions (and meanings, purposes, motives, desires, and so on) were taken to be mental acts in the minds of actors which caused the overt physical movements which the observers could see; as a result, it was thought the *verstehende* social scientist had to ferret out invisible causes and that he could only do this by a special method called 'empathy' in which he relived the lives of those whose acts he wished to explain. By 'reliving' or 'identifying with' his subjects, the social scientist was supposed to be able to discern their mental states and therefore reveal the (mental) causes of the actions he observed. Such an account of social scientific explanation has been rightly criticised,[1] but fortunately this is not an accurate account of *verstehen* explanation, and therefore the traditional criticisms of it which assumed this account miss their mark. This notion of *verstehen* is in error because it is based on a misunderstanding of the ways in which concepts like 'intention', 'meaning', and 'motive' function in our language. These do not refer to occult processes hidden from the view of all but the individual person who is experiencing them and which cause the person's body to move in particular ways, but are rather ways of characterising the actions that we observe. Intentional explanations, for example, make sense of a person's actions by fitting them into a purposeful pattern which reveals how the act was warranted, given the actor, his social and physical situation and his beliefs and wants. An intention is no more 'behind' the action than the meaning of the word is 'behind' the letters of which it is

[1] Cf. T. Abel, 'The Operation called *Verstehen*', and E. Nagel, *Structure of Science*, pp. 480–5.

composed, and it is no more an 'invisble mental cause' of an act than is a melody the invisible cause of the pattern of notes that we hear at a concert.

The arguments supporting this contention would require a recapitulation of Wittgenstein's *Philosophical Investigations* and parts of his *Zettel,* and this is obviously much too difficult and complex to do here. Suffice it to say that the interpretive social scientist offers *verstehen* explanations, that these consist, at the level of individual actions, in demonstrating the *reasons* why a particular act was performed,[2] and that this is accomplished by setting the act within a larger context which includes the aims and cognitions of the actor and the circumstances in which he found himself, which is to say that it is accomplished by using *public* evidence.[3]

However, concentrating on the intentions, etc. of individual actors, even at the level of individual psychology, leads to the mistake of omitting the fundamentally social element inherent in all action descriptions and explanations, and it is this which is of equal or even more interest to the interpretive social scientist. For an action is an action, and a specific action concept can be used, only in the context of a certain set of social rules which provide the criteria in terms of which an actor can be said to be

[2] Thus it is best to think of intentional, etc. explanations as appraisal explanations constructed in the form of a practical syllogism. The sort of explanation appropriate for social science, according to the interpretive model is, therefore, not causal but teleological. For a brilliant philosophical discussion of this, cf. G. H. Von Wright, *Explanation and Understanding*, ch. 3. For an exposition of both the philosophical and methodological aspects of this, cf. R. Harré and P. Secord, *The Explanation of Social Behaviour*. A good example of this approach is H. S. Sullivan, *The Interpersonal Theory of Psychiatry*.

[3] Perhaps the most damaging criticism of the view that intentions are private mental events is the fact that each person is not necessarily the best or sole judge of his own intentions. In discovering the intentions of an act there is no special mental event called an intention which one simply remembers happening; even if one remembers saying to oneself, 'I now intend to do X' this does not guarantee that X was one's intention, for how does one know that one meant what one said except by reference to what one does and the circumstances in which one found oneself, i.e. except by reference to just those considerations which are also available to a third party. One can be deceived about one's intentions just because all intentional explanations involve retrospective interpretations about the point of an act.

performing that action.[4] Thus, one can be described as 'stopping at the traffic light' only in a society which has certain traffic rules, or be described as 'striking out' only if the describer implicitly invokes the rules of baseball. The fact is true not only of conventional action concepts – where it is obviously true, since these concepts implicitly refer to the rules which underlie them – but also of intentional action concepts as well; it is so because one can employ an intentional action concept only by judging that a certain set of basic bodily actions falls within a definite range which counts as doing X, and it is the background of social rules of a particular society which provides the limits of this range, i.e. specifies what is to count as doing X. Thus it is only by reference to certain rules that one can know whether a man is 'horseplaying' as opposed to fighting, waiting instead of loitering. For an action to be of a certain kind it must fall under some description which is socially recognisable as the description of that action because it involves reference to certain social rules.

I want to make this point even more strongly. *These rules*[5] *logically constitute the very possibility of a particular action being said to occur,* which is to say that without the presence of certain rules there can be no action of a certain type. It is for this reason that to describe a person as 'doing X' is thereby to imply that there are rules present in his social order which define what it is to do X and when it is appropriate to do it. Thus, in the absence of certain economic rules one cannot be described as 'buying' or 'selling' in a certain instance (it is this which provides the reason why it would be a mistake to say that 'John *sold* his wife a gift of a watch at Christmas'); and conversely, to describe John as 'selling' is to imply that he is in a special rule-governed situation and is acting accordingly.

Now this set of social rules which is the framework implicitly referred to when one uses an action concept I want to call a

[4] Thus it is that all intentional explanations must be set within a given social context. A good example of this is Weber, *The Protestant Ethic and the Spirit of Capitalism.* Another more readily apparent example is the transactional role-analysis of action to be found in E. Goffman, *The Presentation of Self in Everyday Life.*

[5] 'Rules' refer to expectations of the members of a social group as to what performances are appropriate in a certain situation which itself is definable by means of these rules. Rules refer, therefore, to all socially recognised procedures and standard identifications of situations.

social practice, so that, to sum up what I have said, action descriptions involve implicit reference to social practices. An example of a social practice is the set of rules referred to by the concept 'market-place', so that one might say that the concept 'buying' logically presupposes the existence of the social practice of the market-place. Moreover, just as certain action concepts implicitly contain within themselves a reference to an intention, and just as to understand an action one must understand its intention, so also to understand an action one must understand the practice which it embodies. Another task of the interpretive social scientist is, therefore, to discover the set of rules which underlies a given class of actions, to make these rules explicit, and to relate them to other rules in the society.[6]

But this is not the end of the matter. For if practices constitute the logical possibility of certain classes of actions, then *constitutive meanings* underlie social practices in the same way that practices underlie actions. By a 'constitutive meaning' I mean all those shared assumptions, definitions, and conceptions which structure the world in certain definite ways (hence 'meanings'), and which constitute the logical possibility of the existence of a certain social practice, i.e. without them the practice as defined couldn't exist (hence 'constitutive'). It is only because actors share certain basic conceptions that there can be certain types of social action. For example, the social practice of the market-place can only occur given the shared constitutive meanings of (say) some conception of private property, the notion that in the exchange of goods and services some form of maximising one's own resources is the appropriate course of action, some idea of

[6] This is particularly true of the anthropologist because he is immediately confronted with behaviour which is unintelligible until the rules underlying this behaviour are discovered and explicated. However, this is also an endeavour relevant to sociology and all those other disciplines which study the society of which the social scientist is a member, and this is because the rules by which men act are hardly ever made explicit to them as actors; on this point, cf. H. Garfinkel, *Studies in Ethnomethodology*. Examples of this type of study are the attempt to articulate the rules of price determination in a modern capitalist society (on this, cf. P. W. S. Andrews, *On Competition in Economic Theory*, especially Part 1 which is a review of modern theory), and the attempt to uncover the rules of legislative process in the U.S. Government (on this, cf. the review book of Nelson Polsby, *Congress and the Presidency*). I think that this is also the proper way to view Weber's *Theory of Social and Economic Organisation*.

being an independent agent, etc., etc. Moreover, it follows from this that when one employs a specific action concept in his description of a social activity he thereby, at least implicitly, invokes a set of constitutive meanings as a necessary backdrop in order for this action concept to be used in the first place.

Now constitutive meanings are even less accessible to the social actors involved than are the rules which underlie their actions, for *it is in terms of* these meanings that the actors speak and act. Thus, one can not simply ask the particular actors what the relevant meanings are – as a social scientist might poll people about their beliefs, for example – precisely because it is these meanings which comprise the very language in terms of which people describe and explain themselves, reveal their beliefs and express their attitudes; in order for them to get at these meanings they would have to leave the framework of their ordinary language and experience and look at it 'from the outside', i.e. at least see the possibility of conceptualising themselves in a different way. Here the social scientist is not concerned with what would be the proper thing to do in some context – in which case an ideal informant's word would be privileged – but with understanding the concepts and presuppositions in terms of which something can be said to be what is appropriate. It is therefore a task for the social scientist to attempt to elucidate the meanings which inform specific social practices, and thereby to reveal the structure of intelligibility which accounts for the behaviour he witnesses.[7]

Furthermore, constitutive meanings are obviously not unrelated to one another, and an additional step in explaining a social practice is to relate the constitutive meanings which support it to the other constitutive meanings which underlie the social world of which it is a part, and to see how these constitutive meanings are patterned in such a way as to form a world-view. The purpose in doing this is to discover the *point* a social practice has in a specific society, to see how it fosters the aims and satisfies the needs of the social actors as they themselves define them. Of course, this obviously requires that the social scientist come to terms with a culture's conception of human

[7] For examples of this sort of analysis in social science, cf. S. Beer, *Modern British Politics*; E. and L. Banfield, *The Moral Basis of a Backward Society*; J. Douglas, *The Social Meanings of Suicide*.

needs and purposes, which is to say that he must attempt to grasp the ideas which a certain culture has about the importance which carrying out certain activities may have for a man, its ideas about the sense of human life and what is significant for living it.

The sorts of considerations lead to the conclusion that attempting to set a social practice within the world-view of the social order of which it is a component involves elucidating the basic notions which a people share about the world, society, and human nature. By 'basic notions' I mean such things as a social order's conception of masculinity and feminity; its understanding of the meaning and role of work; its views of nature; its distinctions between public and private; its conception of agency; its ideas about authority, the community, the family; its notion of sex; its beliefs about God and death and so on. In revealing these, the social scientist explains a given social order by articulating the conceptual scheme that defines reality in certain ways, and in terms of which the actions that he views make sense.

Now articulating conceptual schemes has always been regarded as a philosophical activity, and rightly so: for such an enterprise is a conceptual one, attempting to explain the basic presuppositions which underpin and make possible the basic distinctions, responses, and categories of thought and action.[8] An interpretive social science at this level of analysis is a philosophical activity because it attempts to reveal the *a priori* conditions which make social experience in a given society what it is, and it is thus no surprise that the primary examples of this type of social analysis are to be found in political and social philosophy.[9] This is one of the reasons, though not the only one, why philosophy is essential to social analysis, so that the oft-expressed hope of separating out philosophy from social science

[8] This does *not* mean that an interpretive social science is an armchair activity, foregoing empirical research: for even at this level one must be thoroughly aware of the character of social experience before one can reflect on the conditions which make such experience possible.

[9] I have in mind, e.g. Aristotle's *Politics*; H. Arendt's *Human Condition*; A. de Tocqueville's *Democracy in America*; K. Marx's *Grundrisse* and *Economic and Philosophical Manuscripts*; Rousseau's *Second Discourse*; A. Smith's *Wealth of Nations*; and so on. Once again this is an activity long practised in anthropology, cf., e.g. R. Redfield, *The Primitive World and its Transformations*, ch. 4.

is a misguided one; this is also one of the reasons why the classics of social thought continue to have a relevance qualitatively different from that enjoyed by the classics of natural science.

An interpretive social science is one which attempts to uncover the sense of a given action, practice or constitutive meaning; it does this by discovering the intentions and desires of particular actors, by uncovering the set of rules which give point to these sets of rules or practices, and by elucidating the basic conceptual scheme which orders experience in ways that the practices, actions, and experiences which the social scientist observes are made intelligible, by seeing how they fit into a whole structure which defines the nature and purpose of human life. In each of these types of explanation, the social scientist is redescribing an act or experience by setting it into progressively larger contexts of purpose and intelligibility, he reveals *what* the agents are doing by seeing what they are up to and how and why they would be up to that.

4.2 *Its conception of theory and practice*

Just as a positivist social science contains within itself, and is sustained by, a view of theory and practice – the notion of technical control I discussed above – so also interpretive social science is conceptually linked to a notion of theory and practice and is, in fact, partially conceived in terms of this notion. In this section I will first examine its views as to how knowledge from social science is related to human action, and then I will show how these views are defining elements of what constitutes knowledge of social behaviour according to an interpretive social science.

It ought to be clear from the account that I have just given that an interpretive social science is one which reveals to people what it is that they and others are doing when they act and speak as they do. It does this by articulating the symbolic structures in accordance with which people in a particular social setting act, by making clear the criteria of rationality in virtue of which certain alternatives were chosen rather than others, and by revealing the basic assumptions which pattern the world in distinct ways. An interpretive social science uncovers the connections which exist between parts of people's lives, thereby allowing one to see these lives in the whole and enabling one to grasp the significance of particular behaviour in terms of this whole. The result of this sort of analysis is thus a kind of enlightenment in which the meanings of actions, both of one's own as well as of others, are made transparent.

Another way of saying this, and one which leads directly to a discussion of the practical consequences of such a social science, is to draw an analogy with learning a language. Such an analogy is not so far fetched, of course, because speech is itself the paradigm form of social action. Attempting to give an interpretation of social action is like trying to learn a language, for in both one is initially confronted with overt signs (sounds, movements) which are unintelligible and perhaps quite strange, and in both one can only come to understand these signs by learning the rules in accordance with which these signs are expressed, i.e. by relating them to other signs in a systematic and coherent way. Of course, engaging in an exercise of interpretation is even more difficult than simply learning to speak a language because it involves more than just knowing *how* to employ sounds or movements correctly; it also consists in being able to formulate and explain the rules which define what a correct sound or movement is, in being able to relate these rules to one another in a systematic way, and in being able to uncover the conceptual background which structures these formulated rules in a certain way. Nonetheless, it is still true that an interpretation of social action reveals to us its grammar.

The practical upshot of this is that an interpretive social science thereby increases the *possibility of communication* between those who come into contact with the accounts of such a science and those whom it studies. For by revealing what it is that people are doing, i.e. by revealing the rules and assumptions upon which they are acting, it makes it possible for us to engage in a dialogue with them – we understand, as it were, the language of their social life. This is most obviously the case when we are confronted by a foreign culture which, just because we do not understand the rules which govern its peoples' actions or the point of these rules, is cut off from us – we cannot communicate with its members. An interpretive understanding, however, creates the possibility for discourse between us and them by showing us what 'is done' in that society and therefore how to speak and act there. And the same is true within our own culture as well. Coming to understand the ways of so called deviants, learning the 'vocabulary' of children, 'entering the world' of neurotics in therapy, seeing the concerns, hopes and fears of those in different classes and thus grasping the reasons for their apparent odd behaviour, and even uncovering the assumptions by which we ourselves live and thereby perhaps seeing ourselves as related to types or groups of people which we might have thought were radically different from us – all of these are instances in which, by removing the appearance of irrationality or arbitrariness from particular actions, we arrive at a position in which we can speak and act with others.

Moreover, in all of this it is not just being able to communicate with others, but also thereby opening oneself up to their influence, which is significant. For the interpretive social scientist uses concepts to understand beings who define themselves by means of their use of concepts, so that to construct a theory in which one employs new concepts to grasp the sense of one's own or another's social behaviour is to afford people a new means of self-comprehension and thereby to interject new possibilities into their lives. New ways of living become real alternatives when one is able to see the sense of alternative life styles and different ways of looking at the world. At the least one's own assumptions are thrown into relief and therefore one becomes more fully self-conscious; at other times one may well come to redefine oneself and therefore to act differently. To make available a new form of language is to make available a new form of life.

Thus, the knowledge gained from an interpretive social science is useful to men, and can be translated into social life, because it creates the conditions for mutual understanding between different members of the same social order or between members of different social orders, which is to say that it makes possible communication between them where none existed before, or where, if it did exist, such communication was distorted. Moreover, in so far as it opens channels of communication, such knowledge expands the horizons of those who are now able to discourse, because learning how to communicate is learning both new ways of characterising oneself as well as highlighting one's own presuppositions. The aim of an interpretive social theory is to make possible a successful dialogue in speaking and acting between different social actors or within oneself.[10]

Now this notion of theory and practice is not merely appended externally on to the idea of an interpretive social science as is sometimes thought; rather, the two are conceptually connected. For just as possible technical control constitutes the framework within which true knowledge of social behaviour is made possible according to the positivist conception of social science, so for an interpretive social science what can count as a truth is that which creates the possibility for increased communication.

In the first place, the experience which initially gives rise to an interpretive social science is the non-agreement of reciprocal expectations between two acting subjects, so that the aim of such a science is to interpret actions that have blocked communicative interaction in such a way that such interaction becomes possible again. In fact, the relationship between interpretation and communication is even stronger than this; for in an interpretive social science only that which is validated as conceivable or likely by the object of study as a possibly true account of what he is doing can be counted as true, which means to say that *only when both the observer and the actor ultimately come to talk about the actions and beliefs of the actor in the same way is it possible to claim that a correct account has been given.* With regard to ascertaining an agent's purposes and intentions, this point is simply a truistic extension of the phrase 'his purpose'; with regard to the uncovering of social rules, this point is based on the fact that it is our ability to act in the expected and appropriate manner that determines whether we have understood the rules which establish the grounds for communication between socialised individuals; and with regard to constitutive meanings, this point is based on the fact that interpretation attempts to make sense of a particular practice by making explicit what is tacitly assumed by the practitioners, so that we can claim that we have succeeded in uncovering the constitutive meanings only when those who engage in this practice agree that it can be understood in this way – the meanings are meanings *for them,* and whether

[10] One result of this would be to foster a tolerance and respect for others which is an essential prerequisite for a democratic social order; moreover, it would presumably lessen the attractiveness of violence as a way of dealing with those with whom one disagrees.

they are meanings for them can ultimately only be told by them. In each of these three cases, agreement in the concepts used to describe and explain actions and beliefs is a necessary, though obviously not a sufficient, condition for an account to be true,[11] *and this is to say that it is the ability to participate in a communicative interaction which defines what is to count as truth in an interpretive social science.*

I do not mean by this, of course, that the agent can explain his actions better than anyone else – I have already argued against this claim; what I mean is that what the agent does not allow as a reasonable or probable interpretation under the conditions of an uncoerced dialogue cannot be a correct interpretation of what he is doing. Putting it this way, in the context of a dialogue, immediately shows the connection between the criteria of truth in an interpretive social science and its views about how social theory is related to social practice.

4.3 *Some criticisms of this approach*

There are any number of criticisms which might be offered of the foregoing account of the nature of social science and its relation to social practice, but in this section I will confine myself to remarks offered in a positive spirit, i.e. to criticisms that accept the basic foundations that the interpretive model has established, but which argue that the model, taken by itself, is inadequate. For convenience sake I have divided my critical analysis into two main parts, the first dealing with the interpretive theory of social science, the second with its understanding of how theory is related to practice. Of course it ought to be clear by now that I think these two aspects are interrelated with one another, and that I thus make this division for expository reasons only.

The inadequacy of the interpretive model of social science as I have presented it can be seen in at least four different ways. In the first place, such a social science leaves no room for an examination of the conditions which give rise to the actions, rules and beliefs which it seeks to explicate, and, more particularly, it does not provide a means whereby one can study the relation-

[11] In other words, the actors' accepting the theorist's explanation as true is not a conclusive demonstration that the explanation *is* true; rather, it is a necessary prerequisite in order for it to qualify as possibly true.

ships between the structural elements of a social order and the possible forms of behaviour and beliefs which such elements engender. A social scientist will want to investigate not only the meanings of particular types of actions, but those causal factors which give rise to and support the continuing existence of these meanings.

This particular type of analysis may take several different forms. The social scientist may well wish to discover the causes of people adopting certain roles or rule-following activities by examining how a particular social structure constrains its members, delimiting the sorts of activity open to them.[12] Again, he may desire to explain how certain non-social conditions affect the form of social life, for example the ways in which social structure represents an adaptation to the natural environment and the level of technology.[13] Or again, the social scientist may want to uncover the causes of the particular reasons, motives, desires and beliefs which an actor or a group of actors possess, which is to say that he will search for the origins and particular mechanisms through which the surrounding economic, demographic, psychological, political, and religious factors influence the choices that actors make.[14]

In each of these types of analysis the social scientist is attempting to provide *quasi-causal accounts* of the ways in which certain configurations of conditions give rise to certain forms of action, rules, and common meanings. I say 'quasi-causal' rather than causal[15] because, in these sorts of conditionship relations, con-

[12] Cf., for example, E. Goffman, *Asylums*; Meyer Fortes, *Kinship and the Social Order.*

[13] Cf., for example, Lynn White, *Medieval Technology and Social Change.*

[14] Cf., for example, G. W. Thompson, *The Twelve Days.* I take it that it is just this sort of inquiry which the sociology of knowledge undertakes. Cf. P. L. Berger and T. Luckman, *The Social Construction of Reality.*

[15] I adopt this terminology from G. H. Von Wright, *Explanation and Understanding*, ch. 4. I do not mean to imply here that there are no conditionship relations which influence human behaviour and yet operate independently of human will, and which are vital to social scientific explanation. For example, the effect of nutrition on fertility and thus on age distribution levels, and the effect of chemicals on sexual activity, are both instances of genuinely causal explanations of social phenomena. However, the important point here is that in these instances the causal relationships are discovered by natural scientists, and are only employed by social scientists to explain breakdowns

sciousness functions as a mediator between the determining antecedent factors and the subsequent action; in other words, men act in terms of their interpretations of, and intentions towards, their external conditions, rather than being governed directly by them, and therefore these conditions must be understood not as causes but as warranting conditions which make a particular action or belief more 'reasonable', 'justified', or 'appropriate', given the desires, beliefs, and expectations of the actors. Nevertheless, such quasi-causal accounts are a legitimate explanatory device without which a social science would be radically impoverished.

A second type of explanation which the interpretive model neglects is the explanation of *the pattern of unintended consequences of actions*, a feature of social life which, by definition, cannot be explained by referring to the intentions of the individuals concerned. Societies consist of ordered sets of relationships among their members, and it is this basic fact which accounts for the phenomenon that when an action is performed its results rebound throughout the society in ways that are relatively predictable, though the actors themselves might not have been aware of them nor exercise any control over them. It is one job of social science to explore these patterned unintended consequences.[16]

There is one important type of unintended consequence which deserves special mention, namely that which reinforces the actions, beliefs, and roles of the other members of the society such that it 'serves the purpose' of maintaining the structure of the group as a whole. The rules, practices and meanings of a society are structurally interrelated, often mutually reinforcing one another such that they seem to form what might be called a 'system'. This observation is strengthened by the fact that this

in performance or to set the limitations within which the actors must act. For a brilliant example of this, cf. H. Zinnser's *Rats, Lice and History*.

I also do not want to deny that within the class of quasi-causal explanations there may be important distinctions to be drawn, for example, between those changes in conditions which are directly perceived by the actors and those which are only indirectly perceived, or between those changes which lead to an alteration in perceptions and states of the persons and those which lead to an alteration in action without such 'internal' changes. I cannot discuss these subtleties here, unfortunately.

[16] Cf. for example, R. C. O. Matthews, *The Trade Cycle*.

structure remains relatively stable over time despite a constantly fluctuating membership. Because of these facts a social scientist will want to discuss the ways in which social wholes maintain themselves as ongoing systems which persist in an environment, and in this *functional explanations* are invaluable. For a functional explanation attempts to explain a given practice or institution, not by revealing how it arose, nor by disclosing the purposes it is thought to fulfil, but by explaining why it continues to exist, and it does this by demonstrating the contribution its effects make to the continued existence of the social whole which in turn sustains it. A functional analysis uncovers the ways in which the (unintended) consequences of an act or the (unforeseen) effects of an institutional practice modify a host of other social factors, demonstrating how such effects reinforce and strengthen that complex of factors which comprises the social whole, and how, in turn, this complex of factors helps to maintain the original act or practice.[17]

A third way in which the interpretive model is inadequate is that it provides no way for the social scientist to understand structural conflict within a society, that is, it offers no method of analysing the contradictions which might exist between certain actions, rules, and common meanings, or between these and their causes or results. Indeed the problem is worse than this, for an interpretive social science not only fails to give the tools for analysing such situations, but it actually precludes the possibility of identifying such conflicts. The reason for this is that one of the criteria which a good interpretation must satisfy is the demonstration of the coherence which the initially unintelligible act, rule, or belief has in terms of the whole of which it is a part, and this means that, given this standard, the interpreter must assume that the meanings, beliefs, practices, and actions which he encounters are congruent with one another in so far as they are understandable.

This is a fundamental shortcoming, for it means that whole areas of social experience are left out of analysis. What sort of social experience am I referring to? I mean those situations in which people's self-understandings are at variance with their actual social behaviour, so that the way people characterise their

[17] Cf. for example, E. E. Evans-Pritchard's discussion of the function of the blood feud among the Nuer in southern Sudan in *The Nuer*.

activity is in error;[18] in which an actor's ideas and feelings are joined in ways that he is not aware of, and which lead him to act in a pattern which he might not realise and would resent if he knew about;[19] in which a specific belief and action system is incompatible with other stated norms of the culture;[20] in which there are endemic conflicts as the result of conflicts in structural principles;[21] and in which there is a tension within the basic conceptual scheme of a society.[22] In these and other instances what the social scientist wishes to explain is how these discrepancies, incoherences, and contradictions function.

But even more importantly, he will also seek to inquire why they can continue to exist in a given society, and this will lead him to explore the mechanisms which blind agents and thereby enable them to ignore these irrationalities. In this regard, both the ideas and beliefs which social actors have *about* society, as well as the ideas and conceptions which constitute their social reality, may be involved: on the one hand, their theories about society may actually be masking reality in some important way, particularly by obscuring a situation or rationalising it;[23] and on the other hand, particular constitutive meanings of a particular social practice may serve to obscure contradictions between them and other aspects of social life.[24] Here, if one simply tries to

18 Cf. for example, R. Bendix and S. Lipset, *Social Mobility in Industrial Society*, which attempts to demonstrate, contrary to the ethos and beliefs of the whole society, that the U.S.A. does not have a rate of social mobility significantly higher than other industrial societies.

19 Cf. for example, V. Aubert, *Sociology of Law*, ch. 6 which attempts to show that judges' sentencing behaviour is affected by the social class of the accused, though this inconsistency with judicial principles is not recognised by the judges.

20 Cf. Chalmers Johnson, *Revolutionary Change*.

21 Cf. for example, Victor Turner, *Schism and Continuity in an African Society*.

22 Cf. for example, the article by W. Sellers, 'Philosophy and the Scientific Image of Man' in his *Science, Perception and Reality*, in which the tensions between our conception of man as expressed in our ordinary language and as expressed in our scientific language are explored and analysed in a brilliantly insightful way.

23 Cf. for example, C. B. Macpherson, *Possessive Individualism*.

24 For example, in *On the Jewish Question* part of what I take Marx to be claiming is that the universalist norms of the bourgeois legal system and the doctrine of rights in the capitalist political sphere – both of which are rooted in particular conceptions of man and society – function to obscure and rationalise contradictions in the socio-economic order between, on the one

'grasp the intelligibility' of these concepts one will miss the real role which they play in social life.[25]

There is a fourth area of concern to the social scientist, but one again which the interpretive model neglects, and this is the explanation of historical change. For it is also the job of the social scientist to show how a specific institution or social order came to be what it is, and how it will change in determinate ways. An interpretive social science, by methodologically assuming an internal coherence between the self-understandings of the actors, their common meanings, their social practices, and their actions, is unable to explain why it is that a social order will develop – except by invoking external forces – and why it will develop in definite ways. In this regard, all of the types of questions that I have discussed so far will come into play: the actors might well act in a certain way, follow certain rules, and operate in terms of certain constitutive meanings; nevertheless, they might very well also be creating consequences which will in turn affect their needs, interests, and capacities in specific, though to them unknown, ways; they might also come to change their social behaviour as the result of conditions which they themselves have created, though unwittingly; they might be forced to adopt new practices and come to think of themselves in fundamentally new ways because of the contradictions which mark their social arrangements and belief systems, but about which they are unaware. In these and in a myriad of other similar events the social scientist will be interested, precisely because he is interested not only in social order but in social change.[26]

hand, the distribution of goods and conditions of work, and, on the other, the capitalist ideology regarding the equality of opportunity. Such constitutive meanings allow men in capitalist society to claim and to act as if a person's position is a function of his merit and energy (when in fact it is a function of where he started out), and it thereby makes just a situation which on other grounds the society would condemn.

[25] As a good example of this I refer the reader back to the ideological consequences of the belief in the possibility of a policy science which I discussed in section 3.2.

Also, it is interesting to note here how so-called 'ideology-critique' – which many social scientists eschew – is intimately related to the more generally recognised social scientific task of discovering and explaining structural contradictions which generate conflict.

[26] The best example of this is, of course, Marxist historiography. Cf. E. Mandel, *Marxist Economic Theory*.

An interpretive social science is not only inadequate in its account of the nature of social theory, but in its notion of how this theory is related to practice; not surprisingly, these latter difficulties are related to the former ones. I intend here to discuss just two of them.

The interpretive model is inadequate as an account of how social theory is related to social practice because the undistorted communication, which it posits that an interpretive social science will elicit, will most often fail to occur, and this is because the social actors will experience *resistance* (to borrow a Freudian term which is directly applicable here) to the insights of such a science. In order to understand why, it is necessary to grasp the role which ideas about themselves, their social order and other societies play in men's intellectual and emotional lives, and, more specifically, the way in which these ideas are related to the social conditions in which men find themselves. Another way of saying this is that, while the interpretive model promises an increase in communication, it fails to take into account the conditions under which such communication would occur. And this is no accident, for, as I pointed out above, one of the major shortcomings of the interpretive model is its failure to provide a way of understanding the quasi-causal relationship which exists between men and their environment.

A person's ideas about himself and others[27] are never *merely* true or false, abstract statements which he is free to accept or reject simply on the basis of rational argumentation. The reason why this is the case is that these ideas are also ways of coping with the social and natural conditions of his life, they are action-guiding and role supporting. Such ideas are employed to justify to himself and others the particular way of life which he is engaged in living, which means that they make it possible for him to continue living as he does in the situation in which he finds himself. The ideas that he has are deeply ingrained in the way he lives, and the force that such ideas carry for him cannot be appreciated until it is understood exactly what forms this relationship takes.

Moreover, a person learns who and what he is through his early education as he acquires a language, internalises norms, beliefs, values, and attitudes, as he becomes a member of a speci-

[27] What I say here probably applies to our ideas about natural objects too.

fic social group, and this means that his very identity as a person is tied up with the particular world-view of this group and the particular beliefs which are rooted in this world-view. The emotional power which ideas have stems from the fact that such ideas go to the core of what it means to be a person, and it is thus no accident that such ideas are avidly held on to, and that competing interpretations of what one is doing are seen as personally threatening or as ridiculous.

These are some of the reasons why people believe the way they do – and, ironically, these are the very same reasons why misunderstandings and distorted communication between people occur in the first place (because people are unable readily to adopt a 'different viewpoint'). Any political theory which fails to deal with these facts in some appropriate way, which thinks that the simple presentation of ideas will foster a change in social actors' self-conceptions, is naive. The network of communication will only be restored when the problem of resistance is squarely faced.

The second way in which the interpretive model of theory and practice can be criticised is its implicit conservatism. On a superficial level this conservatism manifests itself in the fact, already mentioned, that it assumes an inherent continuity in a particular society, i.e. it systematically ignores the possible structures of conflict within a society, structures which would generate change. This methodological assumption leads to a conservative political theory just because such a science cannot generate any standards of criticism of existing social reality – in fact, it leads one to view the attempt at constructing such standards on the basis of an internal criticism of a social order as misguided.

But the conservatism of the interpretive model is much deeper than this. For such a model makes it appear that all social tensions are rooted in the breakdown of communication between the relevant actors, a breakdown which is itself the result of mistaken ideas that they have about the meaning of their own or another's actions, practices, or beliefs. An interpretive social science promises to reveal to the social actors what they and others are doing, thereby restoring communication by correcting the ideas that they have about each other and themselves. But this makes it sound as if all conflict (or breakdown in communication, for that matter) is generated by mistaken ideas about social reality rather than by the tensions and incompatibilities inherent in this reality itself.

The upshot of this is profoundly conservative, because *it leads to reconciling people to their social order,* and it does this by demonstrating to them that, contrary to their initial beliefs which had caused the breakdown in communication in the first place, actual social practice is inherently rational. In a situation of social conflict and disruption, the interpretive model asserts that the ensuing anxiety and suffering is the result of misunderstandings which, if cleared away, will restore the flow of discourse and hence order – as if such cleavage and breakdown in communication might not result from the irreconcilable demands, interests, needs, and beliefs of the conflicting parties. In a time of upheaval the interpretive model would lead people to seek *to change the way they think about what they or others are doing,* rather than provide them with a theory by means of which they could *change what they or others are doing,* and in this way it supports the *status quo.*

5

The Future: Development of a Critical Social Science

In this concluding chapter I want to follow on from the criticisms of the interpretive model that I have just given, developing a third model of social science and its relation to social life. My remarks will necessarily be sketchy, but it seems to me that it is something like the sort of account I will develop which naturally grows out of the analyses and criticisms that I have made in the earlier parts of this book, and which future arguments in the philosophy of social science will be about.

I call this third account the 'critical model' of social science because of its attempt to integrate theory and practice in its account of the nature of social theory. The critical model is 'critical', as will become apparent, in that it sees theories as analyses of a social situation in terms of those features of it which can be altered in order to eliminate certain frustrations which members in it are experiencing, and its method of testing the truth of a social scientific theory consists partially of ascertaining the theory's practical relevance in leading to the satisfaction of human needs and purposes.

The appellation 'the critical model of social science' is not entirely satisfactory, however; for I do not wish simply to equate it either with the social theory of Marx or with the particular sociological perspective and political stance of the neo-Marxist Frankfurt school. True, Marx's own social science is an exemplar of what a critical social science is,[1] and it is also true that the major philosophical analysis of the concept of 'critical theory' is to be found in the writings of the Frankfurt school;[2] nevertheless, the formal features of this model can easily be detached from the substantive positions which some of its practitioners have adopted, i.e. they do not presuppose any particular theory of social structure and development or a particular conception of human nature.[3] Moreover, the term 'critical theory' has begun to have a wider currency in the social scientific literature,[4] and this seems to justify using this term rather than inventing another one.

Speaking quite generally, a critical social science is characterised by three main features. The first of these is that it accepts the necessity of interpretive categories in social science; in this regard it rests on the arguments in support of the interpretive model which I presented in section 4.1., and it is at odds with the positivist model discussed in Chapter 2. The critical model

[1] I say this even though Marx's own metascientific statements are sometimes positivistic, especially in his later years (cf. for example, the Preface to the second edition of *Capital*). For the ambivalences in Marx's thought, cf. A. Wellmer, *Critical Theory of Society*, ch. 2, and J. Habermas, *Knowledge and Human Interests*, ch. 3. For Marx's analysis of the notion of critique, cf. 'Contribution to the Critique of Hegel's Philosophy of Right. An Introduction', and the 'Theses on Feuerbach'. For an interpretation of Marxist thought which sees it as essentially a critical theory, cf. S. Avineri, *The Social and Political Thought of Karl Marx*, especially ch. 5. For a discussion of the nature of Marxian social analysis along these lines, cf. H. Lefebvre, *The Sociology of Marx*. For an analysis of contemporary society from the viewpoint of Marxism as a critical theory, cf. the work of the Yugoslav philosophers associated with the journal, *Praxis* (in particular cf. S. Stojanovic, *Between Ideals and Reality* and M. Marković, *From Affluence to Praxis*).

[2] Cf. M. Horkheimer, 'Traditional and Critical Theory' reprinted in *Essays in Critical Theory*; H. Marcuse, 'Philosophy and Critical Theory', reprinted in *Negations*; J. Habermas, *Theory and Practice*, *Knowledge and Human Interests*, part 3 and the Appendix entitled 'Knowledge and Interest', and 'The Scientisation of Politics and Public Opinion', in *Towards a Rational Society*; A. Wellmer, *Critical Theory of Society*, ch. 1; and G. Radnitzsky, *Contemporary Schools of Metascience*, vol. 2, chs. 3–7.

[3] Except the important belief that man is an agent and that therefore his behaviour is described by means of action concepts.

[4] Cf. for example, N. Birnbaum, *Towards a Critical Sociology*; the essays by Hymes, Diamond and Scholte in Del Hymes (ed.) *Reinventing Anthropology*; T. Schroyer, 'A Reconceptualisation of Critical Theory' in Corfax and Roach (eds), *Radical Sociology*; Robin Blackburn, *Ideology and Social Science, Readings in Critical Social Theory*.

asserts that in order to have a subject matter at all the social scientist must attempt to understand the intentions and desires of the actors he is observing, as well as the rules and constitutive meanings of their social order. The reason for this is that, as will become clear, a critical theory is rooted in the *felt* needs and sufferings of a group of people, and therefore it is absolutely necessary that the critical theorist come to understand these actors from their own point of view, at least as a first step.

In the second place, a critical social science is one that recognises that a great many of the actions people perform are caused by social conditions over which they have no control, and that a great deal of what people do to one another is not the result of conscious knowledge and choice; in other words, a critical social science is one which seeks to uncover those systems of social relationships which determine the actions of individuals and the unanticipated, though not accidental, consequences of these actions. The critical model is one which requires that its practitioners seek to discover quasi-causal and functional laws of social behaviour in particular social contexts.

The third characteristic of a critical social science is the most important. Such a science is built on the explicit recognition that social theory is interconnected with social practice, such that what is to count as truth is partially determined by the specific ways in which scientific theory is supposed to relate to practical action. This is a conclusion which follows from my analysis in sections 2.2. and 4.2., in which I argued that implicit in a positivist and an interpretive account of social science was a notion of how the knowledge gained from these sciences would be translated into action, and indeed that it was this very notion which was a defining element of what constituted knowledge in these particular models.[5] The critical model takes this hidden

[5] In other words, with regard to these two models I have shown that, first, one of the elements of the epistemological framework which defines what is to count as true knowledge and which consequently defines the basic methodological features of the process of social scientific inquiry is a notion of how theory is related to practice; and, second, that this is the case even though this is only an implicit element in these models, often denied by their practitioners. What I have not done, and what I cannot do in a book of this nature, is to show that this would be the case in *any* model of social scientific knowledge that might be proposed. Such an argument would involve me in an examination of what could count as a scheme of knowledge. Presumably, such an examination would involve an argument to the effect that the criteria that a

connection between theory and practice as one of its starting points, and this means that *it ties its knowledge claims to the satisfaction of human purposes and desires.* Thus the theories of such a science will necessarily be composed of, among other things, an account of how such theories are translatable into action, and this means that the truth or falsity of these theories will be partially determined by whether they are in fact translated into action.[6]

I will turn to this (rather surprising) latter claim in a moment, but first I want to ask the question, how can such a commitment to social practice actually be made part of the *theory* of a social science? It is at this point at which my earlier discussion of the identification of structural conflict within a society, as well as of the explanation of historical change in a dialectical manner, becomes pre-eminent. For a critical social science can fulfil its task of showing how its truths are to be translated into practice by employing the quasi-causal and functional 'laws' which it discovers to explain the contradictions in social life which them-

claim would have to meet in order to be counted as a claim to knowledge would necessarily include some reference to the way in which such putative knowledge claims were to affect man's interrelationship with, and activity in, the world. On this, cf. N. Rescher, *The Primacy of Practice*; G. Radnitzsky, *Contemporary Schools of Metascience*, vol. 2, ch. 2; J. Habermas, *Knowledge and Human Interests.*

Nevertheless, even though I have not accomplished this, enough has already been said to justify proposing a model of social science which makes the connection between theory and practice explicit and central.

[6] I say 'partially determined' because, among other reasons, a theory might be constructed but then lost before it was disseminated, and one would hardly want to claim that, because it never affected social life, it was therefore false. A critical social theory is one which offers an account of future social developments and how they will occur partially because of the existence of this account itself, and if, as a result of the account's not becoming known, the social order develops along lines other than the theory predicted, then the truth of the theory is indeterminate.

Furthermore, just because some people for whom the theory is directed accept its interpretation of their situation and act accordingly, this only supports the claims to truth by the theory without actually validating it as true. All those involved must accept it under appropriate circumstances in order for it to be true.

Moreover, I say 'partially determined' also because there are obviously other requirements that must be met in order for a theory to be true, among them: the theory must be internally consistent; it must be formulated according to rules which permit intersubjective evidence and testing of claims, and it must be in agreement with this evidence; and it must be compatible with other claims acknowledged to be true, i.e. it must be theoretically solvent.

selves underlie the tensions and conflicts the scientist observes, and which are experienced by the social actors in certain specific ways. This involves an attempt to develop a historical account which reveals how it is that the relevant social actors came to be what they are, i.e. it will try to show how and why these actors have the particular purposes and needs that they have, and, at the same time, how and why these purposes and needs are unsatisfied. The critical social scientist is one who seeks to disclose how the historical process was such that the social order which he is examining was incapable of satisfying some of the wants and needs which it engendered, and in so doing he will have accounted for the structural conflict and accompanying social discontent which he perceives.

It is important to note that the explanations which result from such an approach would always be in terms of the *felt* needs and *experienced* privations or sufferings of the agents involved. The reason why this is the case is that the critical theorist operates in terms of the same assumption as does the interpretive social scientist, namely, that human actions and systems of actions are rooted in the self-understandings, perceptions, and intentions of the actors involved, so that it is in terms of these – though not these exclusively – that one must understand human actions. All explanations of actions must refer to the phenomenological experience of the actors; this is obviously true when considering their intentions, rules and common meanings, but it is also true with regard to the more naturalistic looking explanations – as I pointed out in Chapter 4, they are only *quasi*-causal.

So a critical social science is one which attempts to account for the sufferings and felt needs of the actors in a social group by seeing them as the result of certain structural conflicts in the social order, and it seeks to explain these conflicts – and hence the sufferings and felt needs – by giving a historical account in quasi-causal terms of the latent contradictions between the sorts of needs, wants, and purposes which the social order gives rise to and the sorts of (inadequate) satisfactions which it provides. Such a social science tries to show that it is only by conceptualising the social order in the way that it suggests that one can comprehend the dissatisfactions which the members of this order experience.

At this point in the analysis, perhaps an imaginary, and

obviously simplistic, illustration would be helpful.[7] Let us say that a critical theorist wished to focus his attention on the dissatisfactions that women feel in western industrialised societies. His explanation of these dissatisfactions might look like this: certain (specified) changes in the production and distribution of goods and services in industrial societies have resulted in a (specified) radical alteration in the sort of time and effort involved in doing domestic work, and such an alteration has led to housewives having little to do in the house. However, industrial societies are also marked by features which prevent the housewife from doing anything else; such features include everything from highly restrictive union shops to value systems which declare that it is unfeminine to work and to compete with men. These features are related to those circumstances which gave rise to the changes in the production and distribution in the first place in the following manner . . . (here, some high level theory would have to be invoked or created). It is the conjunction of these two sets of circumstances which is responsible for the internal conflict which women suffer at a certain level of social development.

I will return to this example in a moment; first it is necessary to ask, how is such a science practical? Obviously, for it to be so its theories must not simply explain the sources and nature of discontent experienced by the social actors, but also must demonstrate how it is that such discontent can be eliminated by removing, in some specified way, the structural contradictions which underlie it. This means that the quasi-causal explanations which are given must be related to the felt needs and sufferings of the social actors *in such a way that they show how these feelings can be overcome by the actors coming to understand themselves in their situation as the product of certain inherent contradictions in their social order, contradictions which they can remove by taking an appropriate course of action to change this social order*. A critical social theory is meant to inform and guide the activities of a class of dissatisfied actors which has been brought

[7] As will be evident, the illustration is not wholly imaginary. However, I prefer to call it imaginary because I intend what I say as a mere indication of the sorts of things a critical theory does, not as a full-blown exemplar of such a theory. Moreover, I do not know of any single work which does all of the things that I claim a critical theory must do with regard to this matter (although Simone de Beauvoir's profound *The Second Sex* should be read in this regard).

into existence by social agencies which it claims can only be comprehended by this theory, and it does so by revealing how the irrationalities of social life which are causing the dissatisfaction can be eliminated by taking some specific action which the theory calls for.

How the practical intent of critical theory is accomplished can be seen by examining the ways in which it deals with the problem of resistance which I discussed above; it does so in a threefold manner. The first way is actually an attempt to bypass the problem, for a critical social theory, because it is rooted in the experience of thwarted desires and repressed needs, seeks to demonstrate that the actors can rid themselves of *their own dissatisfaction* only by acting in a way specified by the theory. In other words, the theory is not a moralistic or utopian one which attempts to get people to simply adopt a new set of ideas which are foreign and threatening to them, but rather is one which seeks to articulate the felt grievances of a specific group of actors, to provide a vocabulary in virtue of which they and their situation can be conceptualised, to explain why the conditions in which they find themselves are frustrating to them, and to offer a programme of action which is intended to end with the satisfaction of these desires. Thus, because of these aims, the theory must be translatable into the ordinary language in which the experience of the actors is expressed, and it must speak to the felt needs of these actors, with the result that a critical social theory must be grounded in the self-understandings of the actors even as it seeks to get them to conceive of themselves and their situations differently.

The second way that a critical social theory overcomes resistance, and therefore can be practical, is through what is called ideology-critique. For one element in a critical theory will be an attempt at demonstrating that the beliefs and attitudes which the actors have are incoherent because internally contradictory, or that their self-understandings are deficient because they fail to account for the life experiences which the actors themselves have. In other words, an integral part of a critical social science is the demonstration of exactly in what ways the ideologies of the social actors are illusions, with the ideas that such a demonstration will strip these ideologies of their power; it tries to show men how they have been deceived, given their experiences, aims, and desires, and in the process it seeks to reveal to them the rational way of going about getting what they really want.

But even here the rooting of the social science in the self-understandings of the actors is evident. For precisely because their ideas function as ways of helping them to cope with their situation, the contradictory or inadequate ideas which particular actors do have about themselves and their social order must also contain clues as to their true situation: their ideas cannot be *merely false*, but rather they must also contain an intimation of their real needs. The critical theorist must therefore show how the manifest content of the actors' ideas mask a latent content which is what reveals the true meaning of these ideas, and which is therefore the source of their power over those who hold them. In this way ideology-critique is not merely a negative activity, for it not only seeks to point out the error in the ideas men have and the way this error helps to maintain a social order which is thwarting to them, but it also attempts to reveal the truth which these ideas contain by demonstrating how they point to an important dimension in the psychological economy of their proponents, and how they suggest a new self-conception which makes explicit what they only implicitly contained. It is only by providing an alternative which speaks to the disguised but real needs which underlie the (illusory) ideas of the actors that the resistance of these actors to a new conception of themselves and their situation can be overcome.

But, of course – and this leads to the third way in which resistance is dealt with in this model of theory and practice – a social science which is explicitly founded on an awareness of the ways in which certain conditions can cause certain beliefs will also be aware that ideas and self-understandings may be illusions which are necessary in order to sustain a particular form of living. Consequently, a critical social science must be prepared for the situation in which the people to whom its theories are directed might reject these new interpretations of their situation even when such interpretations are grounded in their self-understandings, and even when these interpretations uncover the real content of these understandings in the process of showing them to be incoherent or inadequate.

This difficulty is met by a critical theorist elaborating in his theory on the ways in which social conditions will change, so that the illusions which actors have about themselves will no longer have the significance that they presently have. In other words, the theory must offer an account which shows that the social structure will alter in ways which will undermine the appropriateness of the (false) ideologies which the actors of this structure possess.[8]

The problem of resistance is overcome, therefore, by a coming together of two factors, both of which are necessary and neither of which is independent of the other. These two factors are, on the one hand, specific changes in the structure of society, and, on the other, a theory which makes sense of these changes in terms of the real needs of those who are involved in them. It is this conjunction which a critical theorist must attempt to develop in his overall theory: on the one hand, an account of the basic changes in a social order (changes which will make the social actors more amenable to his ideology-critique), and, on the other, an ideology critique which seeks to articulate the real grievances and aspirations of a specific class of people even as it attempts to demonstrate the illusory character of their ideas (an ideology critique which itself will contribute to changes in the social order which the theory anticipates).[9]

[8] Of course, the theorist does not believe that these changes in the social structure are wholly independent of the existence of his theory; rather, the theory is itself the catalytic agent which sparks social change by revealing to actors, given their developing situation, how they ought to act.

[9] Here I am discussing the resistance the group under study may put up against a certain analysis of itself, but *not* the resistance which other groups in the society may have to *it*. Thus, although I show here how the imposition of the theory by those convinced of it on to the rest of the group (as in the case of the 'vanguard of the proletariat') is ruled out in a critical theory approach, I do *not* discuss the possibility of the group imposing its will on to other groups which are opposed to it in the way the theory says, and which resist it. So it is that the problem of eliminating manipulative domination in political life, while dealt with on one level, returns at another.

Obviously it is not possible to develop a full political theory here, and this is what would be required to discuss adequately this second type of resistance; however, in the light of the idea of educative transformation I discuss below, and especially in the light of my remarks there that it is the institutionalisation of free and uncoerced communication which is the vision that underlies the critical model, I think that the direction which such a political theory would take is clear. I submit that it would be a theory which explained how opposition could be overcome, in the appropriate circumstances, by creating the conditions for open communication through a combined policy of moral suasion, the refusal to submit to commands, and the elimination of possible

Perhaps returning to the example of women's liberation will help in clarifying the additional components required of a critical theory if it is to fulfil its intention of being truly practical. An analysis of the dissatisfactions of women according to the model of critical theory as I have outlined it would not only contain the sorts of statements that I mentioned above, but these would be combined with a critique of the self-understandings of contemporary women; an account of the dynamics of the social situation in which they find themselves in such a way that it would become possible for women to alter their self-understandings and their social situation; and a programme of action. So that, for example, a critical theory would contain, besides the analysis given earlier, the following: a detailed and extensive attempt to articulate the felt dissatisfactions of women, their boredom, their sense of uselessness, their resentment, etc.; a criticism of the basic ideas in terms of which women define themselves, attempting to show both that these ideas are not coherent (e.g. that they define what fulfilment means for a woman in such a way that a modern woman could never be fulfilled) or appropriate (e.g. that they contain a picture of women that is irrelevant to the experience and demands of modern life), but that they also contain intimations of what a woman really needs and wants (to be responsible, in control of her life, to be active, etc.); a theory of social dynamics which would indicate the ways in which the social order is changing in such a way as to undermine the basic ideas which women now have of themselves (e.g. that the economy is expanding in specified ways which require that increasing numbers of women work, that increasing educational opportunities will force women to see the irrelevance of their inherited values, that changes in birth control techniques will allow radically different sexual behaviour, and so on); and lastly, an analysis of the sorts of action which women might take in order to achieve the satisfaction the theory claims they are really seeking, and thereby eliminate the suffering which was the touchstone of the theory in the first place (e.g. that women ought to form 'consciousness-raising' groups, that they ought to work to

reprisals. In this regard, it is Gandhi who becomes the most significant political theorist, for it is just this sort of theory which he develops in the context of mass society. On all of this, cf. J. V. Bondurant, *The Conquest of Violence*.

change certain laws, that they ought to forsake certain sorts of sexual relationships, and so on).

At this point a critical commentator might offer an extremely powerful objection to the foregoing analysis; it is one which has to do with the ways in which the 'appropriate courses of action' called for by the theory are undertaken. For he might claim, the critical model is supposedly one at odds with the positivist model presented in Chapter 2, and yet there has been no argument presented so far which would preclude an instrumentalist understanding of the ways in which a critical theory is to be translated into practice. In fact, so his objection might run, in so far as a critical social science produced quasi-causal laws, it would be providing the basis upon which, through the manipulation of certain variables, a certain set of actions and beliefs could be produced (assuming that the intentions and other beliefs of the actors remained relatively constant). The conclusion of the critic might be, therefore, that, for all its talk of integrating theory and practice, from the practical view-point the critical model is essentially no different from the positivist model![10]

Now this is an important objection, but it overlooks a fundamental point; this is that the translation of a critical social science into practice would necessarily require the participation and active involvement of the social actors themselves in this process. The reason why this is so is because such a science is composed of an interpretive element, and therefore its theories can only be validated in the self-understandings of the actors themselves. That this is the case may perhaps best be seen by examining the *two* ways in which theory can be translated into practice according to the critical model; in each of them it will be

[10] Indeed, it is just this type of consideration which underlies the (mis)uses of Marxism by Leninist and Stalinist parties. These parties have a fundamentally instrumentalist conception of Marxist theory and its relation to political practice. It is their idea that it is up to them, having attained enlightenment and a correct understanding of their objective situation, to seize power and manipulate the social order in specified ways in order to bring those in whose name they are acting to a proper understanding of themselves (i.e. to an acceptance of the Party).

For a theoretical justification of this instrumentalism by someone who also grasps the difference between a positivist and a critical social theory, cf. Georg Lukács, *History and Class Consciousness*, especially the essays, 'Critical Observations on Rosa Luxembourg's "Critique of the Russian Revolution",' and 'Towards a Methodology of the Problem of Organisation'.

clear why it is that, given the nature of a critical social science, a purely manipulative use of the knowledge gained from this science is impossible.

The first way that the critical model envisages that its theories will become part of social life is through what I want to call the *educative role* of social theory.[11] According to this educative conception, the function of the social scientist is not to provide knowledge of quasi-causal laws to a policy scientist who will determine which social conditions are to be manipulated in order to effect a particular goal, but rather *to enlighten the social actors so that, coming to see themselves and their social situation in a new way, they themselves can decide to alter the conditions which they find repressive.* In other words, the social scientist tries to 'raise the consciousness' of the actors whose situation he is studying.

What is involved in this process of increasing self-consciousness? There are two crucial elements here. The first of these is the attempt by the social scientist to provide the means whereby the actors he is studying can come to see themselves in ways radically different from their own self-conceptions. By offering a theory which explains why it is that they are frustrated and unsatisfied, why they are doomed to continue in this condition given their conception of themselves in their social order, and why it is that they have the images of themselves which they do have, the social scientist tries to show to the actors that, as long as they define their needs and wants as they do, and as long as they see themselves as relating to their social order as they do, they will remain thwarted and repressed. Moreover, he also offers an alternative conception to them of what they are, attempting to demonstrate how their frustrations can be overcome only if they are conceptualised in a certain way, only if the actors related their experiences to one another in a manner which they themselves had not thought of, or pursued goals different from those which they were pursuing, or adopted novel courses of action. In this, as I mentioned earlier, the social scientist will offer his alternative formulations of people's needs and wants in

[11] For a most interesting account of this educative role of critical theory, with special reference to the peasants in an underdeveloped country, cf. Paulo Freire, *Pedagogy of the Oppressed.*

terms of the latent content of the self-conceptions which the actors themselves have.

But this process of social actors rethinking what it is they desire and how these desires are related to the objects they pursue and the actions they undertake, i.e. coming to define what they are differently, is only one element in the process of increasing self-consciousness. The other element has to do with enlightening them as to the precise mechanisms which combine to frustrate them, but about which they had been ignorant and which therefore operated independently of their will. The social scientist reveals to the relevant actors how particular quasi-causal relationships determine that their social situation be repressive, even though they did not know that these relationships were the reason for their frustration, and he thereby indicates to them which aspects of their social situation they can alter in order to improve their lot. A critical social science is one which discloses to the actors it studies how an aspect of their social life, which they did not know was a determining element of their social experience, had been an element of that life all along, and it thereby provides the means by which these actors can become clear to themselves.

These two facets of the process of making the lives of the social actors transparent to themselves are obviously interrelated. The first element, which consists in the actors coming to have different pictures of themselves, and therefore redefining their needs and desires, can occur only because the social scientist is able to demonstrate that the social order is characterised by specific quasi-causal relations such that, given their self-conceptions, and attendant wants, the actors will be inevitably frustrated. And the second element, which consists of learning the ways in which the social order is repressive and therefore the kinds of action they must undertake in order to emancipate themselves from it, is only comprehensible in light of the new self-definitions which the theory calls for.

That the goal of a critical social science, according to this view, is the enlightenment of the actors it studies distinguishes it fundamentally from the positivist model I discussed earlier. For the purpose of instrumental manipulation along the lines of a policy science is an attempt by men at getting certain set relationships to work for them so that they may achieve a certain end efficiently, whereas the purpose of education in terms of the knowledge provided by a critical social science is the transformation of the consciousness of the actors it seeks to understand, a transformation which will increase their autonomy by making it possible for them to determine collectively the conditions under which they will live.[12] In the former, an elite determines rational courses of action for the group by knowing certain natural necessities, whereas in the latter all the members of the group actively engage in deciding what it is they are and want, and what arrangements must be altered or established in order to fulfil themselves.[13]

The second way in which theory may be translated into practice according to the critical model is through an instrumental application of its quasi-causal laws. But even here there are fundamental differences between the way the knowledge from a positivist social science would be instrumentally applied and the way the knowledge from a critical social science would be instrumentally applied.

The first and less important difference which I have in mind is the attitude which the implementor of knowledge would have in acting in accordance with the critical model in contrast to the positivist model. Because it explicitly assumes that all (quasi-) causal relationships in the social world rest on the intentions,

[12] I do not mean to imply here that a policy scientist might not also try to change people's ideas and beliefs; indeed, one of the prime tasks of a policy scientist presumably would be to attempt to convince people that the course adopted was the only rational alternative open, given the laws of the social order. But this should not be confused with the process of 'raising consciousness': for changing people's ideas to make them do what the policy scientist wants is different from changing their ideas so as to increase their capacity to make informed and rational choices. The policy scientist could only seek to change certain beliefs about how the social world operated, whereas the critical social scientist as educator would attempt to get people to see that the social world need not operate as it does, that it is open to change by them.

[13] Of course the particular ways that members of the group can interrelate with one another, i.e. ways in which they can organise themselves so that members can practically participate in the process of education and collective determination of courses of action, cannot be ascertained apart from the concrete situation of a specific case. Thus, whether a political party, a union, a 'consciousness-raising group', a collective, and so on, is appropriate will depend on the theory and on the circumstances.

This educative conception of theory and practice leads directly into the Aristotelean conception of politics I discussed in section 3.1.

beliefs, purposes, and values of the actors which comprise it, if one were acting in terms of the critical model in manipulating variables in accordance with these (quasi-) causal laws in order to foster a policy, one would necessarily know that these laws themselves could be changed (because the actors might develop new purposes and values), i.e. that one might refuse to act as they dictate. This means that, in deciding to act in accordance with these laws as they are revealed by a critical social science, the policy-maker would at least implicitly be *making a choice* which expresses his reading of the *status quo* and his attitudes towards it. Here, therefore, there would be no question of impartially acting in terms of the necessary conditions of social life; of letting 'the truth' about a social order determine political actions; of neutrally seeking what is the case and structuring social life in accordance with it, in just the way that men build bridges in terms of the 'givens' of the natural world as revealed by natural science – all attitudes which characterise the policy scientific approach. Instead, there would be at least the implicit recognition that choosing to act in accordance with the basic structural components of one's society was itself an act of at least implicit political evaluation.

The second and more important difference between an instrumentalist conception of the critical model and such a conception of the positivist model has to do with the role which the actors in the name of whom the policy expert is working play in the process of decision-making. For in contradistinction to the positivist account, according to the critical model there must exist a constant critical interchange between the policy expert and the actors who will be affected by his decisions. Just because the theory which supports the expert's analysis in the critical model is one which seeks to relate quasi-causal social conditions to the felt needs of the actors in such a way that these felt needs will be satisfied, this model requires that the policy expert consult the actors in the first instance, and continue to consult with them throughout the entire operation of attempting to technically control particular social situations. The reason for this is that the results of the various manipulations recommended by the policy expert can only be judged effective by referring to the opinions of the ordinary actors in whose name these manipulations are taken, and this is because the articulation of needs and their satisfaction can only be confirmed in the consciousness of the social actors themselves. According to the critical model, then, a 'policy science' can only proceed from the world of the social actors and it must lead back to it.

Of course this relation between expert and actors is not the simple one-way street that I paint here, for the opinions of the actors in their original, frustrated state reflect illusions that they have about themselves; an expert acting in terms of a critical theory would, therefore, also have to engage in a process of educating his subjects. A critical theory is one that attempts to explain the ignorance that people have not only about their social order but about their needs and wants as well; it attempts to explain their willingness to accept repressive and unsatisfying social conditions because they have a mistaken understanding of who and what they are. The quasi-causal laws in a critical theory are set within a nexus which includes an ideology-critique, such that accepting the truth of the theory involves coming to define oneself and what it is one thinks one needs and wants, in a way quite different from what one had done before. It is only thus that the satisfaction that the critical theorist promises will occur, not simply when the conditions of people's lives are changed, but when their understanding of themselves is changed in specific ways as well. All of this means that the policy expert must try to persuade those in whose name he is acting to adopt a new picture of themselves, to interpret their experiences differently.

But such an educative process is also one of interaction, as the policy expert must re-evaluate and alter his interpretations of the actors he is dealing with as they express their thoughts and aspirations, as they react to and reflect on the new self-understanding which he is attempting to get them to adopt. So that just as the expert must be constantly revising his estimations of the appropriateness of the technical advice he gives as to which conditions to alter in light of the responses of the actors affected by it, so he must also be responsive to their reactions to his attempts at getting them to conceptualise themselves differently.

The democratic implications of this view ought not to be ignored. This model requires that there be a free flow of natural and uncoerced expressions from the actors to the experts and vice versa, and this kind of discourse can only occur when the population is free from domination or threat. This kind of ideal communication situation can be institutionalised only in the democratic form of public discussion among the citizenry.[14] Ironically, as with the notion of a policy science, the critical account also wishes to bring the political order into harmony with the ideal of science; but here the similarity ends, for the critical theorist understands science as a system of free and unrestricted communication, rather than as a body of objective truths in terms of which society ought to be run, and it is this notion of open discussion, and the uncurbed expression of opinions and desires, which it both presupposes and seeks to foster.

How different all of this is from the conception of a policy science developed out of the positivist model of social science. In that conception there is no requirement that the policy expert refer to the public expression of needs and wants; there is no idea that the expert must continually be in communication with the public, and indeed that he must change his recommendations on the basis of this communication; and there is no prerequisite of a democratic political order required for his work to be possible. In fact, a policy science is an elitist and anti-democratic programme designed to eliminate just those features of political decision-making which the critical model deems essential.

This emphasis on the involvement and participation of the relevant social actors in the implementation of the knowledge gained from a critical social science – an emphasis found in both the 'educative role' and the 'expert role' which such a social science might play in social life – is no accident. For the critical model envisages a social science which speaks to the actors which it studies, which attempts to provide a means whereby they can solve the problems which are facing them, *and whose truth is thereby judged partially on the basis of whether or not the satisfactions which it promises are forthcoming.* It follows from this that the objects of study of this science – the social actors about which it seeks to provide an understanding – actually help to determine the truth of this science's theories by

[14] In other words, the *second* way that the knowledge gained from a critical social science might be translated into action – i.e. instrumentally – can only occur in a fully democratic setting. Outside of this setting, a critical theory is translatable into practice only in the educative mode I discussed above.

their reaction to them. According to the critical model, one criterion of the truth of social scientific claims is the response which these people make to these claims, and it is for this reason that the application of its purported truths requires a central and determining role for the actors who are to be affected by it.

So here we do have a philosophy of social science which makes the self-conscious integration of theory and practice its central core; this can be seen in the way in which a critical theory arises and develops, and in the manner in which its claims are validated. As to its origin, a critical theory is clearly rooted in concrete social experience, for it is one which is explicitly conceived with the practical intention of overcoming felt dissatisfaction. Consequently, it names the people for whom it is directed; it analyses their suffering; it offers enlightenment to them about what their real needs and wants are; it demonstrates to them in what way their ideas about themselves are false, and at the same time extracts from these false ideas implicit truths about them; it points to those inherently contradictory social conditions which both engendered specific needs and make it impossible for them to be satisfied; it reveals the mechanisms in terms of which this process of repression operates; and, in the light of changing social conditions which it describes, it offers a mode of activity by which they can intervene in and change the social processes which are thwarting to them. A critical theory arises out of the problems of everyday life, and is constructed with an eye towards solving them.

As to its development, a critical theory is not a static doctrine, a fully completed set of laws which are simply applied to, or imposed on concrete situations; rather, it is corrected and reformulated as it continually confronts the practical men it seeks to enlighten. A critical social theory is not divorced from social practice in the sense of being set over and against it as a blueprint to be followed; here, the objects of the theory actually become subjects of it, which is to say, they help to fashion it by their own choices and actions, and by their responses to it.

And lastly, the claims of such a theory can only be validated partially in terms of the responses that the social actors themselves have to the theory. This is to say that whether it indeed offers a way out of an untenable situation (and is therefore a true theory) is partially determined by whether those for whom it is written recognise it as a way out and act on its principles. It is an internal – and decisive – criticism of any critical theory if it is rejected by the people to whom it is addressed.

According to the critical model of social science, a social theory does not simply offer a picture of the way that a social order works; instead, a social theory is itself a catalytic agent of change within the complex of social life which it analyses.

Such, in broad outline, is the sketch of a model of social science which takes explicit account of the relationship between theory and practice, and which, at the same time, is consistent with the sorts of philosophical analyses which I offered in Chapter 4. In offering this model I hope to have been participating in the creation of that humanist synthesis of the analytic tradition and continental thought which I mentioned earlier.

Be that as it may, I hope that in this book I have at least demonstrated that there are indeed various competing ways of conceptualising the manner in which we are to understand social behaviour, and that these different conceptualisations are intimately related to the political question of how our understanding of social life affects, and ought to affect, our living of it. Furthermore, I hope that, on the basis of this demonstration, I have shown that no account of the nature of social science can be adequate unless it takes explicit cognisance of its political ramifications. The philosophy of social science cannot be severed from political philosophy any more than social theory can be severed from social practice.

Whatever is the case, it is surely obvious that my remarks, while perhaps suggesting the direction for future thought, are no substitute for it. Many of the points I have made require more argument than I have offered, and they demand more probing of the crucial yet unsolved or unmentioned philosophical problems which lie behind them. It is to these, and to the development of a substantive theory of social life that will help to emancipate men from repressive social structures under which they now live, that we must turn our future attention.

Bibliography

Throughout the book, with each critical argument or historical position I have tried to cite what appeared to me to be the crucial relevant source, often with comments. In this bibliography, therefore, I simply list all the works which are mentioned in the text, and I refer the reader to the appropriate place in the text for an indication of how a specific work fits into the general thesis I have offered. For clarity's sake I have divided the bibliography into two sections: the first which consists of works relevant to the development of the philosophical arguments I have made, the second which consists of works in social science cited as instances exemplifying points in these arguments. Also, it should be mentioned that I have confined myself to books which are readily available and which are in English.

A. WORKS RELEVANT TO THE PHILOSOPHICAL ARGUMENT REGARDING THEORY AND PRACTICE

Abel, T., 'The Operation Called *Verstehen*', *American Journal of Sociology*, 54, 1948–9, pp. 211–18.

Apel, K. O., 'The *A Priori* of Communication and the Foundation of the Humanities', *Man and World*, vol. 5, no. 1, Feb. 1972.

——— *Analytic Philosophy and the Geisteswissenschaften* (D. Reidel, Dordrecht, Holland, 1967).

Arendt, H., *The Human Condition* (University of Chicago Press, 1969).

Aron, R., *Eighteen Lectures on Industrial Society* (Weidenfeld & Nicolson, London, 1961).

——— *The Industrial Society* (Praeger, New York, 1967).

Avineri, S., *The Social and Political Thought of Karl Marx* (Cambridge University Press, 1969).

Bacon, F., *Novum Organum* and the *New Atlantis*, in *Selected Works* (Encyclopedia Britannica (Great Books), Chicago, 1955).

Beauvoir, S. de, *The Second Sex* (Penguin, Harmondsworth, 1972).

Bell, D., *The End of Ideology* (Free Press, New York, 1960).

Bendix, R., *Social Science and the Distrust of Reason* (University of California Press, Berkeley, 1951).

Bernstein, R., *Praxis and Action* (Duckworth, London, 1972).

Birnbaum, N., *Towards a Critical Sociology* (Oxford University Press, 1971).

Blackburn, R., *Ideology and Social Science. Readings in Critical Social Theory* (Fontana/Collins, London, 1972).

Bondurant, J. V., *The Conquest of Violence* (University of California Press, Berkeley, 1969).

Borger, R. and Cioffi, F., *Explanation and the Behavioural Sciences* (Cambridge University Press, Cambridge, 1970).

Brodbeck, M., 'Explanation, Prediction, and "Imperfect" Knowledge', in Feigl & Maxwell (eds), *Minnesota Studies in the Philosophy of Science*, vol. 3 (University of Minnesota Press, Minneapolis, 1962).

Catlin, George E. G., *The Science and Method of Politics*, (Kegan Paul, Trench & Trubner, London, 1927).

Chardin, T. de, *The Phenomenon of Man* (Fontana, London, 1965).
Comte, Auguste, 'The System of Positive Polity. A Plan of the Scientific Operations Necessary for Reorganising Society', in Congreve and Hutton (trans.), *The System of Positive Polity*, vol. 4 (Longmans, London, 1877), and in Fletcher (ed.) *New Science and New Society, Early Essays* (Heineman, London, 1973).
——— *The Positive Philosophy of Auguste Comte*, freely trans. by H. Martineau (Kegan Paul, Trench & Trubner, London, 1875).
Condorcet, Antoine Nicolas, *Sketch for a Historical Picture of the Progress of the Human Mind*, trans. J. Barraclough (Weidenfeld & Nicolson, London, 1955).
Crick, B., *The American Science of Politics* (Routledge & Kegan Paul, London, 1959).
Dray, W., *Laws and Explanation in History* (Oxford University Press, 1957).
Durkheim, E., *The Division of Labour in Society* (Free Press, New York, 1947).
——— *The Elementary Forms of Religious Life* (Allen & Unwin, London, 1968).
——— *Professional Ethics and Civic Morals* (Routledge & Kegan Paul, London, 1957).
——— *The Rules of the Sociological Method* (Free Press, New York, 1965).
——— *Socialism and Saint-Simon* (Kent State University Press, 1958).
——— *Sociology and Philosophy* (Cohen & West, London, 1953).
Emmett, D., *Functions, Purposes and Powers* (Macmillan, London, 1972).
Feyerabend, P. K., 'Against Method', in Radner and Winokur (eds) *Minnesota Studies in the Philosophy of Science*, vol. 4 (University of Minnesota Press, Minneapolis, 1970).
——— 'Consolations for the Specialist' in Lakatos and Musgrave, *Criticism and the Growth of Knowledge* (Cambridge University Press, 1970).
——— 'Explanation, Reduction, and Empiricism', in Feigl and Maxwell (eds) *Minnesota Studies*, vol. 3 (University of Minnesota Press, Minneapolis, 1962).
Friere, P., *Pedagogy of the Oppressed* (Sheed & Ward, London, 1972).
Galbraith, J. K., *The New Industrial State* (Penguin, Harmondsworth, 1968).
Gellner, E., 'Concepts and Society', in *Transactions of the Fifth World World Congress of Sociology*, 1962, and reprinted in Wilson (ed.), *Rationality*, (Blackwell, Oxford, 1973).
Goldman, L., *The Human Sciences and Philosophy* (Jonathan Cape, London, 1969).
Habermas, J., *Knowledge and Human Interests* (Heinemann, London, 1972).
——— *Theory and Practice* (Beacon Press, Boston, 1973).
——— *Towards a Rational Society* (Heinemann, London, 1971).
Hanson, N., 'On the Symmetry between Explanation and Prediction', *The Philosophical Review*, 68, 1959.
Harre, R. and Secord, P., *The Explanation of Social Behaviour* (Blackwell, Oxford, 1972).
Hayek, F. A., *The Counter-Revolution of Science* (Free Press, New York, 1955).
Hempel, Carl, *Aspects of Scientific Explanation* (Free Press, New York, 1965)

Horkheimer, M. and Adorno, T., *Dialectic of Enlightenment* (Herder & Herder, New York, 1972).
Horkheimer, M., *Critical Theory* (selected essays) trans. O'Connell (Herder & Herder, New York, 1972).
——— *The Eclipse of Reason* (Oxford University Press, 1947).
Hymes, D. (ed.), *Reinventing Anthropology* (Random House, New York, 1969).
Kolakowski, L., *The Alienation of Reason* (Doubleday, Garden City, 1968).
Korner, S., *Categorial Frameworks* (Blackwell, Oxford, 1970).
——— *Experience and Theory* (Routledge & Kegan Paul, London, 1966).
Kuhn, T., *The Structure of Scientific Revolutions* (University of Chicago Press, 1970).
Lakatos, I., 'Falsification and the Methodology of Scientific Research Programmes', in Lakatos and Musgrave (eds), *Criticism and the Growth of Knowledge* (Cambridge University Press, 1970), pp. 91–195.
Lasswell, H., 'Policy Sciences', in the *International Journal of the Social Sciences*, (Macmillan, New York, 1968), pp. 181–89.
——— *A Pre-view of Policy Sciences* (Elsevier, London, 1971).
——— *Psychopathology and Politics* (University of Chicago Press, 1930).
Lefebvre, H., *The Sociology of Marx* (Penguin, Harmondsworth, 1972).
Lipset, S. M., *Political Man* (Heinemann, London, 1960).
Lobkowicz, N., *Theory and Practice: History of a Concept from Aristotle to Marx* (University of Notre Dame Press, 1967).
Louch, A. R., *Explanation and Human Action* (Blackwell, Oxford, 1967).
Lukács, G., *Class and Class Consciousness* (M.I.T. Press, Cambridge, Mass., 1971).
Lundberg, George, *Can Science Save Us*? (Longmans Green, New York, 1947).
Lynd, Robert S., *Knowledge for What: the Place of Social Science in American Culture* (Princeton University Press, 1939).
MacIntyre, A., 'A Mistake about Causality in Social Science', in Lasslett and Runciman (eds), *Politics, Philosophy and Society*, vol. 2 (Blackwell, Oxford, 1962).
——— 'The Idea of a Social Science', *Supplementary Proceedings of the Aristotelian Society*, 41, 1967, pp. 95–114. Reprinted in MacIntyre, A., *Against the Self-Images of the Age* (Duckworth, London, 1971).
Mannheim, Karl, *Ideology and Utopia* (Routledge & Kegan Paul, London, 1966).
Manuel, F., *The New World of Henri Saint-Simon* (University of Notre Dame Press, 1963).
Marcuse, H., *Negations* (Penguin, Harmondsworth, 1972).
——— *One Dimensional Man* (Abacus, Tunbridge Wells, 1972).
Marković, M., *From Affluence to Praxis* (University of Michigan Press, Ann Arbor, 1973).
Marx, K., 'On the Jewish Question', 'Contribution to a Critique of Hegel's Philosophy of Right. An Introduction', 'Theses on Feuerbach', all in Easton and Guddat (eds), *Writings of the Young Marx on Philosophy and Society* (Doubleday, Garden City, 1967).

Marx, K., 'Preface to the Second Edition', *Capital*, trans. Moore and Avelling (Allen & Unwin, London, 1946).
Medawar, P., *The Art of the Soluble* (Methuen, London, 1967).
Mill, J. S., *A System of Logic* (Longmans, London, 1970).
Mills, C. Wright, *The Sociological Imagination* (Oxford University Press, 1959).
Moon, J. D., 'The Logic of Political Inquiry: A Synthesis of Opposed Perspectives', in F. Greenstein and N. Polsby (eds), *Handbook of Political Science*, vol. 1 (Addison-Wesley, Reading, Mass., 1974).
Morgenbesser, S., 'Is it a Science?' in A. Macintyre and D. Emmett (eds) *Sociological Theory and Philosophical Analysis*, (Macmillan, London, 1970).
Musson, A. and Robinson, E., *Science and Technology in the Industrial Revolution* (Univ. of Toronto Press, 1969)
Nagel, E., *The Structure of Science* (Routledge & Kegan Paul, London, 1961).
Partridge, P. H., 'Philosophy, Politics, Ideology', in A. Quinton (ed.), *Political Philosophy*, (Oxford University Press, 1962).
Popper, Karl, *Conjectures and Refutations* (Routledge & Kegan Paul, London, 1969).
——— *The Logic of Scientific Discovery* (Hutchinson, London. 1959).
——— *The Open Society and its Enemies* (Routledge & Kegan Paul, London, 1966).
——— *The Poverty of Historicism* (Routledge & Kegan Paul, London, 1957).
Radnitzsky, G., *Contemporary Schools of Metascience* (Henry Regnery, Chicago, 1970).
Rescher, N., *The Primacy of Practice* (Blackwell, Oxford, 1973).
Riley, G., *Values, Objectivity, and the Social Sciences* (Addison-Wesley, Reading, Mass., 1974).
Rossi, P., *Philosophy, Technology and the Arts in the Early Modern Era* (Harper and Row, New York, 1970)
Saint-Simon, Claude Henri de, *Selected Writings*, ed. F. W. Markham (Blackwell, Oxford, 1952).
Scheffler, I., *Science and Subjectivity* (Bobbs-Merrill, Indianapolis, 1967).
Schroyer, T., 'A Reconceptualisation of Critical Theory', in Corfax and Roach (eds), *Radical Sociology* (Basic Books, New York, 1971).
Schutz, A., *The Phenomenology of the Social World* (Heinemann, London, 1972).
Scriven, M., 'Explanation and Prediction in Evolutionary Theory', *Science*, 130, 1959.
Sellers, W., 'Philosophy and the Scientific Image of Man', in *Science, Perception and Reality* (Routledge & Kegan Paul, London, 1963).
Shils, E., 'The End of Ideology', *Encounter*, Nov. 1955.
Simey, T. S., *Social Science and Social Purpose* (Constable, London, 1968).
Skinner, B. F., *Beyond Freedom and Dignity* (Knopf, New York, 1972).
——— *Walden II* (Macmillan, New York, 1948).
Stojanovic, S., *Between Ideals and Reality* (Oxford University Press, 1973).
Storing, H. (ed.), *Essays on the Scientific Study of Politics* (Holt, Rinehart & Winston, London, 1963).
Taylor, C., *The Explanation of Behaviour* (Routledge & Kegan Paul, London, 1964).

Taylor, C., 'Interpretation and the Sciences of Man', *Review of Metaphysics*, Sept. 1971, pp. 3–50.
Turgot, R., *Notes on a Universal History*, in Stephans (ed.) *Life and Writings of Turgot* (Longmans Green, London, 1895).
Ward, Lester, *Psychic Factors in Civilisation* (Ginn, Boston, 1893).
Weber, M., *From Max Weber*, eds Gerth and Mills (Routledge & Kegan Paul, London, 1952).
——— *On Methodology of the Social Sciences*, (ed.) E. Shils (Free Press, New York, 1949).
——— *The Protestant Ethic and the Spirit of Capitalism* (Allen & Unwin, London, 1958).
——— *The Theory of Social and Economic Organisation*, (ed.) T. Parsons (Free Press, New York, 1964).
Wellmer, A., *Critical Theory of Society* (Herder & Herder, New York, 1971).
Wilson, B. (ed.), *Rationality* (Blackwell, Oxford, 1973).
Winch, P., *The Idea of a Social Science* (Routledge & Kegan Paul, London, 1958).
——— 'Understanding a Primitive Society', in B. Wilson (ed.), *Rationality* (Blackwell, Oxford, 1973), and in Peter Winch, *Ethics and Action* (Routledge & Kegan Paul, London, 1972).
Wittgenstein, L., *Philosophical Investigations* (Blackwell, Oxford, 1953).
——— *Zettel* (Blackwell, Oxford, 1968).
Wolin, S., 'Paradigms and Political Theories', in King and Parekh (eds), *Politics and Experience* (Cambridge University Press, 1968).
——— *Politics and Vision* (Little Brown, 1960).
Wootton, Barbara, *Testament for Social Science* (Allen & Unwin, London, 1950).
Wright, G. H. Von, *Explanation and Understanding* (Routledge & Kegan Paul, London, 1971).

B. WORKS USED AS EXAMPLES OF CERTAIN POINTS IN THE ARGUMENT

Andrews, P. W. S., *On Competition in Economic Theory* (Macmillan, London, 1964).
Aubert, V., *Sociology of Law* (Institute for Social Research, Oslo, 1964).
Banfield, E. C. and Banfield, L. F., *The Moral Basis of a Backward Society* (Free Press, New York, 1958).
Beer, S., *Modern British Politics* (Faber & Faber, London, 1965).
Bendix, R. and Lipset, S. M., *Social Mobility in Industrial Society* (University of California Press, Berkeley, 1959).
Berger, P. L. and Luckman, T., *The Social Construction of Reality* (Penguin, Harmondsworth, 1971).
Douglas, J., *The Social Meanings of Suicide* (Princeton University Press, 1967).
Evans-Pritchard, E. E., *The Nuer* (Oxford University Press, 1956).
Fortes, M., *Kinship and the Social Order* (Routledge & Kegan Paul, London, 1970).
Garfinkel, H., *Studies in Ethnomethodology* (Prentice-Hall, Hemel Hempstead, 1967).
Goffman, E., *Asylums* (Penguin, Harmondsworth, 1970).

Goffman, E., *The Presentation of Self in Everyday Life* (Penguin, Harmondsworth, 1971).
Johnson, C., *Revolutionary Change* (University of London Press, 1969).
Macpherson, C. B., *Possessive Individualism* (Oxford University Press, 1962).
Mandel, E., *Marxist Economic Theory* (Monthly Review Press, New York, 1969).
Matthews, R. C. O., *The Trade Cycle* (Cambridge University Press, 1959).
Polsby, N., *Congress and the Presidency* (Prentice-Hall, Hemel Hempstead, 1964).
Prest, A. R. and Turvey, R., 'Cost-Benefit Analysis: A Survey', in *Surveys of Economic Theory* (Macmillan, London, 1967).
Redfield, R., *The Primitive World and its Transformations* (Penguin, Harmondsworth, 1968).
Sullivan, H. S., *The Interpersonal Theory of Psychiatry* (Norton, New York, 1953).
Thompson, G. W., *The Twelve Days* (Hutchinson, London, 1964).
Turner, V., *Schism and Continuity in an African Society* (Manchester University Press, 1957).
White, L., *Medieval Technology and Social Change* (Clarendon Press, Oxford, 1962).
Zinsser, H., *Rats, Lice and History* (Bantam Books, London, 1971).

Index